GLOBALISED.
CLIMATISED.
STIGMATISED.

Globalised. Climatised. Stigmatised
©2019 Camillo M. Gonsalves

Printed in the United States

ISBN#9781092338172

This is the fourth volume in a series entitled
Caribbean Ideas
published by Strategy Forum, Inc.
Kingstown, St. Vincent and the Grenadines

Other titles in the series include
The Case for Caribbean Reparatory Justice
Our Caribbean Civilisation and Its Political Prospects
Our Caribbean and Global Insecurity

GLOBALISED. CLIMATISED. STIGMATISED.

Camillo M. Gonsalves

Thank you to Karen, Selah, Micah, and Italia

Contents

Me little, but me talawah

-The Pioneers

INTRODUCTION

Resistance, Resilience, and Small Island Exceptionalism

"We little but we talawah" is a Jamaican expression whose usage — thanks to reggae and dance hall music — has been exported across the Caribbean. It means, roughly, that we are small, but we are strong and resilient. It has long been colloquial shorthand for an inchoate type of exceptionalism in the Caribbean. That exceptionalism has been cited to explain individual achievement rather than regional character. Look! The tiny Caribbean birthed three Nobel laureates![1] Usain Bolt is the world's greatest sprinter! Garfield Sobers is the greatest cricketer! We little, but we talawah!

But the Caribbean's outsized influence on sports and culture, and the litany of legendary individuals that have planted the flags of superlative Caribbean achievement in diverse pursuits across the globe, are mere manifestations of a more fundamental truth: that the islands of the Caribbean are different. The constraints of small size, the backdrop of a complex history, the confluence of cultures and races, the geopolitical imperatives and the geographic and topographical realities have conspired to produce societies and nations that exist beyond conventional frames of reference or forecasting models. By those conventions, be they economic, political or sociological, the countries of the Caribbean are not viable. They should not exist as independent nations.

But here we are. Surviving, thriving even, in a geopolitical order that neither anticipated nor accounted for our existence.

The nations of the Caribbean are *sui generis*. And while the precise ingredients of their uniqueness are not replicated elsewhere on the planet, they do share enough basic similarities with some small states scattered across the Atlantic, Indian and Pacific Oceans to discern a common small island exceptionalism. This exceptionalism is not in the triumphalist, "we're #1" vein of today's manifestations of jingoistic great power exceptionalism, nor is it simply the "island mentality" or "small island syndrome" born of isolated navel-gazing and limited horizons. Instead, small island exceptionalism spans regions and civilisations. It is shaped by the practical realities of smallness, of islandness, and of the delicate dance of alternately accommodating, resisting and adapting to tremendous exogenous pressures. Through this dance, small island states have forged a personality and developmental outlook without parallel in any other group of countries in the world.

This collection of essays argues that this uniqueness — this small island exceptionalism — is indispensable to any analysis that considers the past, perspective or path of independent small island states. We are islands first. We fit neatly into no other paradigm. Our achievements and aspirations cannot be understood without first understanding this obvious, but often overlooked fact.

Political thought, economic theory and the prescriptions applied or imposed on small island states have gradually moved beyond yesteryear's "one-size-fits-all" orthodoxy. However, there is a persistent belief that analyses and advice can simply be scaled down — almost mathematically — from other experiences and mechanically applied to the small island context.

This is folly. Just as "one-size-fits-all" is inapplicable, so too is "one-concept-fits-all".

There are 33 independent small island states that enjoy membership in the United Nations. Collectively, they are home to 40 million people and have a gross domestic product of US $650 billion. These rough measures of political weight, population and economic power point to a need for greater study, analysis and understanding of small island states, as seen through their own eyes and the prism of their unique circumstances and exceptional nature. In attempting to advance such an island-centric discourse, this publication primarily relies on Caribbean experiences and examples — probably an odd choice in support of an argument for pan-island commonality and solidarity. However, the hope is that what is lost in generality is outweighed by gains in focus, and that future writers will expand upon the reach and scope of these humble observations.

Globalised. Climatised. Stigmatised.

The global entrenchment of neoliberal orthodoxy as our planet's guiding philosophical underpinning, and the erection of its corresponding financial architecture on the foundations of monopoly capitalism, represent the gilded cage that confines the developmental aspirations of small islands. Like much of what ails our global village, island states played little role in constructing the cage we now inhabit. The two decades of decolonisation that freed most islands states to govern their own affairs spanned the 1960s to 1980s. By that time, the Bretton Woods system was firmly entrenched, and its attendant World Bank and International Monetary Fund were well established as the carrot and stick of economic development. Most islands were in their infancy as independent nations when Ronald Reagan and Margaret Thatcher were forcefully elaborating the contours of a new geopolitical order that remains in effect today, with few modifications. By the time we became independent, the system was set.

However, it is fair to say that there is nothing to suggest that a radically different system would have emerged if islands had been given the opportunity or voice at the nascent stages of our current neoliberal epoch. At the time of independence, we witnessed an ascension of local middle classes into the roles formerly occupied by colonial masters. However, the new political elites adopted a cautious, incrementalist approach to altering the fully-formed colonial structures that were bequeathed to island states. The faces had changed, but, to quote the colloquialism of the day, it was the 'same ole khaki pants'. Most of those who imagined an alternative to the prevailing orthodoxies failed to find favour at the polls, and those who formed government through less conventional methods were quickly ostracised, demonised and neutralised by forces well beyond our seas.

The pre-independence global order, and islands' tacit acceptance of its strictures as a precondition to nationhood, has evolved into a massive system of rules and enforcement mechanisms that do not consider or accommodate island specificities. Global arbiters of policy seek to impose an ideological homogeneity through force of law, might and money. These externally imposed prescriptions are a terror, and the chilling effect that they have on creative policy solutions has constrained most islands to follow an orthodoxy prescribed from on high.

The contradictions and constraints of those policies and practices have caused island states to suffer the unholy trinity of being globalised, climatised and stigmatised to varying harmful degrees. This trinity of anti-island action has produced some cruel socioeconomic paradoxes, including:

- The smallest contributors to climate change are the most affected.

- The lowest contributors to terrorist financing or banking impropriety are the most constrained.

- The smallest producers of global goods and services are most restricted by the rules of international trade.

- The most indebted are among the least likely to get debt relief or concessional financing.

These paradoxes, and the systems that produced them, pose existential threats to the sustainability of island states. However, today, there is little popular appetite for quixotic quests by small island states to revolutionise or reinvent the global socioeconomic order. Pragmatic reform is the order of the day.

There is real potential for carefully selected pragmatic reforms to improve lives and alter the islands' developmental trajectory. These pages contain a few modest suggestions, including changes related to diplomacy, development assistance, poverty reduction, and productive economic sectors. It suggests changes in the way islands are viewed, which would in turn result in changes to their policy choices. "We little but we talawah" is a description, not a development policy, or a justification for global indifference. This publication argues for reforms to ensure that islands remain indomitable, but never ignored.

CHAPTER ONE

Life Over Debt

Unnu old vampire
Only trod upon creation
Sucking the blood of the nation
Unnu set of vampire

- Peter Tosh

Debt is a social and ideological construct, not a simple economic fact. Furthermore, as understood long ago, liberalization of capital flow serves as a powerful weapon against social justice and democracy. Recent policy decisions are choices by the powerful, based on perceived self-interest, not mysterious "economic laws." Technical devices to alleviate their worst effects were proposed years ago, but have been dismissed by powerful interests that benefit. And the institutions that design the national and global systems are no more exempt from the need to demonstrate their legitimacy than predecessors that have thankfully been dismantled.[2]

- Noam Chomsky

In late 2009, on the eve of general elections in Saint Kitts and Nevis, then-Prime Minister Dr. Denzil Douglas infamously responded to opposition criticisms that the Federation's astronomical debt to GDP ratio of 200% was proof positive of gross economic mismanagement. Addressing a pre-election public rally, Prime Minister Douglas leaned into the microphone and exclaimed dismissively: "They come talking stupidness 'bout public debt. Public debt mi arse!" Douglas was comfortably re-elected to office, notwithstanding conventional hand wringing about the magnitude of the debt and predictions that the country would enter the ranks of failed states.

Today, the Kittitian public debt-to-GDP ratio has plummeted to 60%, meeting the prudential target of the Eastern Caribbean Central Bank a decade ahead of schedule. It repaid its US $73 million loan from the International Monetary Fund (IMF) well before the due date. A decade after Douglas' colourful comments went viral in the region, a new school of economic thought known as Modern Monetary Theory suggests that governments borrowing in their own currency should be unconcerned with fiscal constraints; while economics professors and a former United States Treasury Secretary point to America's projected 105% debt to GDP ratio and shrug it off, saying "it's time for Washington to put away its debt obsession and focus on bigger things"[3] — a position that is essentially a measured academic restatement of Dr. Douglas' colloquial thesis.

This reconsideration of pubic debt is of more than passing significance to small island developing states. Debt is as much a feature of small island states as beaches, and the public debt-to-GDP ratio has been fetishised as a key indicator of fiscal health. The most recent 2018 data found Barbados, Jamaica, Seychelles, and Singapore at or above debt-to-GDP ratios of 100%, while another one third of African, Caribbean or Pacific islands were burdened by ratios above 65%. The low debt outliers, which include Haiti, the Marshall Islands, the Maldives, or Solomon Islands, are often the beneficiaries of special bilateral relationships or multilateral debt relief schemes like the Highly Indebted Poor Countries (HIPC) initiative.

Interestingly, while the Bretton Woods institutions can rattle off the public debt-to-GDP ratios of any nation, a request for them to provide information or analysis on the scope of private consumer or household debt as a proportion of GDP is likely to illicit only blank stares. Despite the fact that the 2008 crisis and the 1990s crash in Japan were caused in large part by rapidly ballooning private debt, the neoclassical arbiters of economic health continue to blithely ignore the unsustainable private credit binges that regularly precipitate these disasters.[4] Among small island states, evidence suggests that credit and remittance-fuelled consumption is growing far more rapidly than government debt and is a greater predictor of economic or banking instability than the well-worn public debt-to-GDP metric.

Nonetheless, public debt is not an insignificant economic indicator, and the debt-to-GDP ratio is not a useless measure. However, the questions about debt revolve around its primacy as a driver of economic policy, the varying causes and consequences of high debt in the small island context, and the quest for a workable multilateral solution to high levels of indebtedness among islands — particularly those classified as middle- and high-income countries.

As a candidate for the presidency of the United States, Donald Trump once proclaimed "I love debt. I'm the king of debt[5]." When he later clarified that "I've always loved debt, I must be honest with you. I don't love it for countries but I love it individually[6];" Trump was speaking to the special stigma attached to nations' public debt as opposed to corporate debt. At least part of the stigma is fuelled by stereotypes of inefficient governments wasting taxpayers money on ill-conceived white elephants and corruption.

Debt, Austerity and the Paradox of Thrift

In October 2012, over the course of three pages of charts and graphs in their *World Economic Outlook*,[7] the IMF made a startling admission that sent shock waves through the economic world:

"Sorry, we were wrong about austerity."

Keynesian economists and academics did a smug victory lap of I-told-you-sos. Mainstream press outlets like *Bloomberg*,[8] the *Economist*,[9] *Business Insider*,[10] the *Washington Post*[11] and the *New York Times* weighed in on the stunning mea culpa. However, for whatever reason, the IMF bombshell exploded without incident among island states, even though the not-so-invisible hand of the IMF is tightly around the throat of many island economies, imposing austerity prescriptions based on assumptions that the IMF itself is calling invalid.

In the 2012 *World Economic Outlook*, the IMF asked itself a seemingly innocuous question: "Are We Underestimating Fiscal Multipliers?" The answer was yes. In summary, the IMF confession is based on their misreading of the size and impact of fiscal "multipliers". Economists try to figure out the effect that particular types of spending or consolidation will have on GDP. If the multiplier is small, then austerity is not that painful and stimulus is not that effective. If the multiplier is large, then the opposite is true.

For example, if you have a large multiplier, of, say, 1.5, it would mean that if you increased government spending by 1%, GDP would increase by 1.5%. This would be a pro-stimulus multiplier, because the GDP would grow at a rate that exceeds government spending. However, the IMF had been basing its economic prescriptions and projections on a multiplier of about 0.5. This meant that if you reduced spending by 1%, your GDP would only shrink by half that much. With a multiplier of 0.5, there is a mathematical argument in favour of austerity. The closer the multiplier gets to, or exceeds, 1, the weaker that mathematical argument becomes (this is ignoring all of the broader economic, ideological, social, and political anti-austerity arguments). Similarly, with a multiplier of 0.5, stimulus isn't that efficient, because a 1% rise in government spending would yield a mere 0.5% increase in GDP.

It turns out that the IMF multiplier estimate of 0.5 was completely groundless. In the October 2012 *World Economic Outlook*, they confess that "our results indicate that multipliers have actually been in the 0.9 to 1.7 range since the Great Recession". Other economists have suggested that, in current conditions, the multiplier is actually around 2. Simply put, the IMF's unjustified and uninformed assumptions abut multipliers forced a counterproductive austerity on countries, which deepened and lengthened the global crisis.

This is an absolutely stunning admission of guilt by the IMF, and one that reinforces Keynes' famous statement in every Economics 101 textbook that "the boom, not the slump, is the right time for austerity at the Treasury".

But the IMF went further. It concluded its *mea culpa* by saying "More work on how fiscal multipliers depend on time and economic conditions is warranted." In other words, multipliers (and by extension, the impact of austerity) depend on context, and the IMF doesn't have the necessary contextual data. For island states, serious analysis of fiscal multipliers in small, open, island economies with a limited production base, inability to dictate terms of trade, small private sector, and large public service is non-existent — particularly within the context of the aftermath of the global economic and financial crisis.

The IMF followed-up the October 2012 *World Economic Outlook* with an even more shocking piece of self-analysis. In a 2013 paper called "Greece: Ex Post Evaluation of Exceptional Access under the 2010 Stand-By Arrangement,"[12] the IMF took a look back at the debacle that was their 2010 austerity package, which almost completely destroyed a Greek economy already battered by the economic crisis. After recognising the "notable failures" of the IMF package, the paper looks into why their proposed prescriptions almost killed the patient. One of the main reasons that the Greek policy failed, according to the paper, was that the IMF grossly underestimated just how much economic damage would be caused by austerity in that context.[13] (Interestingly, their other main finding was that they (and the EU) should simply have acknowledged from the start that Greece would not be able to repay its debt, and that major debt forgiveness should have been in place from the outset).

A 2013 IMF Working Paper called "The Challenge of Debt Reduction during Fiscal Consolidation"[14] makes an interesting, if obvious point:

> Studies suggest that fiscal multipliers are currently high in many advanced economies. One important implication is that fiscal tightening could raise the debt ratio in the short term, as fiscal gains are partly wiped out by the decline in output.

What this means is that austerity is a highly questionable course of action in the current economic climate for countries with high debt levels. What will happen, essentially, is that imposing cuts in this climate will result in an *increase* in the debt-to-GDP ratio. The reasoning, stripped from the mathematical mumbo-jumbo, is basic and intuitive: austerity will shrink weaker economies and reduce the GDP. Smaller GDP means greater debt-to-GDP ratio.

The impact of this worsening debt-to-GDP ratio is potentially calamitous. According to the IMF:

> [Raising the debt ratio] could be an issue if financial markets focus on the short-term behaviour of the debt ratio, or if country authorities engage in repeated rounds of tightening in an effort to get the debt ratio to converge to the official target.

Imagine that you are the minister of finance of a small, indebted country with a weak economy in the midst of the ongoing economic crisis. Imagine that you subscribe to an austerity programme with the goal of reducing debt and/or increasing investor confidence. According to the IMF, a very real possibility is that the opposite will happen: your economy may shrink too rapidly, resulting in a deteriorating debt ratio. That shrinking economy and ballooning debt will make financial markets and credit ratings agencies jittery, resulting in credit downgrades and less favourable loan terms. The financial markets will then tell you, as minster of finance, that your debt-to-GDP is out of whack because of "structural" problems in your economy. You will also be told that your problem is a "lack of investor confidence". The solution they may well propose: more austerity. Thus, the spiral begins, and "repeated rounds of tightening in an effort to get the debt ratio to converge to the official target" becomes a grim socioeconomic and political nightmare.

Austerity, Structural Adjustment and the Washington Consensus were largely unchallenged conventional wisdom when these policies were being applied to strangle growth and ferment social unrest in poor and developing countries. When the global economic and financial crisis hit, the expectation was that these same policies would be applied with equal strictness to "advanced" economies in Europe and Asia. However, all of a sudden, when the problems of austerity showed up in the cities and governments where IMF economists actually lived and worked, the IMF suddenly became introspective, reflective and rigorous in testing its assumptions and formulae. The "revised" conclusion is now that austerity may not be such a good thing after all. Of course, the IMF economists try to insulate themselves by saying austerity is not a good thing "in advanced economies," suggesting that the concept may still have utility in the developing world. But that distinction is also false, and born of a paternal arrogance that assumes profligacy and corruption in developing countries, and that values a rich European's economic discomfort as more real and tragic than the suffering of poor peoples.

Good Debt vs. Bad Debt

Even the most cursory analysis of the debt of Small Island Developing States reveals that its recent growth has been driven not by extravagant wastefulness or errant policy decisions, but rather exogenous shocks — primarily weather related — that have exacerbated the underlying structural weaknesses inherent in smallness and islandness. Other external shocks, like the world economic and financial crisis, severely constrained demand in major trading markets, crippled tourism revenues, and necessitated countercyclical, debt-fuelled stimulus to keep island states out of economic free-fall.

The contribution of disaster recovery, preparation and climate adaptation to the expansion of debt in some island states has been massive. In Saint Vincent and the Grenadines, the every-other-year drumbeat of seemingly minor storms, floods and droughts have caused loss and damage averaging 10% of GDP per event over the last decade. On the other end of the spectrum, Dominica suffered US $1.5 billion damages and losses from Hurricane Maria in 2017, a whopping 226% of GDP.[15] Those damages caused a massive 14% contraction[16] in the Dominican economy in 2018. A mere two years before Hurricane Maria, Dominica was pummelled by Tropical Storm Erika, which caused losses and damages amounting to 90% of the Dominican GDP.[17] The price tag for clean-up, reconstruction and infrastructural adaptation will undoubtedly exceed the tiny revenue base of Dominica's 75,000 people.

Additionally, the cost of post-colonial developmental catch-up has also been enormous in island states that existed for hundreds of years as heavily-exploited outposts for the generation of colonial wealth. Former Grenadian Prime Minister Maurice Bishop once observed that colonialism was an "ordeal that left us with only one secondary school built by the colonialists after 300 years of colonial rule".[18] In the 45 years of Grenada's post-colonial existence, it has been required to build over 20 additional secondary schools to adequately meet its population's educational needs. This is one small indication of the developmental abyss encountered by island states on day one of their lives as independent states. By and large, these necessary investments in education, health, and public infrastructure have required governments to borrow. Indeed, within the confines of the current global order, the developmental disadvantage bequeathed by colonialism in the vast majority of island states would be impossible to address without aid and loans. These legitimate loans have contributed to islands' public debt-to-GDP ratios, and unfortunately, to the erroneous perception that those ratios represent profligacy. Going forward, the urgent policy goals of adapting to climate change, stimulating growth, achieving the Sustainable Development Goals and simultaneously reducing the debt burden cannot be attained without a coordinated program of island-specific development assistance that includes both additional borrowing and substantial reductions in existing public debt.

Budgetary Priorities and Fiscal Space

The fixation on the public debt-to-GDP metric and its accompanying pride of place in the list of budgetary priorities must be revisited in this era of low interest rates, low inflation and urgent developmental priorities. For example, in Saint Vincent and the Grenadines, the bulk of its external debt is dominated by highly concessionary soft loans from the Caribbean Development Bank, the World Bank, Taiwan, and Venezuela. As such, the Vincentian external debt is typically low interest, with lengthy times to maturity.[19] To equate today's Vincentian debt-to-GDP ratio to one of two decades ago, when interest and inflation rates were higher, and maturity times shorter, would be misleading, at best. Similarly, the overriding priority accorded to debt reduction — both as a matter of local budgetary policy and externally-imposed structural adjustment — must be revisited.

Today, higher public debt burdens do not affect private investment or economic growth in the same ways as hitherto. A far greater threat to growth is draconian austerity. The impact of high debt to GDP ratios in today's economic circumstances is uncertain. According to Lawrence Summers, former U.S. Treasury Secretary and Director of the U.S. National Economic Council, "[i]n truth, no one knows the benefits and costs of different debt levels — 75 percent of GDP, 100 percent of GDP, or even 150 percent of GDP".[20] Summers and Jason Furman, former Chair of the White House Council of Economic Advisors and current Professor of Economic Policy at Harvard University, argue instead that

> *Much more pressing are the problems of languishing labour force participation rates, slow economic growth, persistent poverty, a lack of access to health insurance, and global climate change. Politicians should not let large deficits deter them from addressing these fundamental challenges.*[21]

The politicians and governments of small island developing states should consider the extent to which they can apply this advice in their local contexts.

The more useful measure of the extent to which debt acts as drag on development in island states is the degree to which fiscal space is constrained by debt servicing. According to the Jubilee Debt Campaign, a UK-based non-profit, average government external debt payments increased from 6.7% of government revenue in 2014 to 9.7% of government revenue by 2016.[22] Of the 24 so-called middle-income members of the Alliance of Small Island States for which data were available, the average was 10.4%. For those AOSIS members considered "upper middle-income," the average was 12.1% — well above the global average. Many AOSIS members, like Grenada, Fiji and Jamaica, were devoting more than 20% of revenue to servicing external debt. More than a simple debt-to-GDP average, these proportions suggest that islands' fiscal space may be more constrained by debt service than other developing countries. This lack of fiscal manoeuvrability — particularly when climate change demands increased public expenditure on infrastructure — demands a focussed effort on debt relief for island states.

Island-Specific Debt Relief

Small Island Developing States have been at the forefront of advocating debt relief for "Highly Indebted Middle Income Countries" (HIMIC). Recently, Jamaica, in particular, has led the charge on this initiative.[23] Styled after HIPC,[24] the similar, long-running debt relief programme for Highly Indebted Poor Countries, the validity of the arguments in favour of HIMIC relief are not in dispute. However, in casting the definitional net so widely as to include all "middle income countries," the framers of the HIMIC initiative have maximised their potential base of political support while simultaneously making it unpalatable to the lending institutions responsible for granting debt relief. According to the World Bank, there are 103 middle-income countries in the world[25] that are home to five of the world's seven billion people and almost three-quarters of those classified as poor. The real and potential debt burdens of large middle income countries, like Mexico, Turkey and South Africa — to say nothing of behemoths such as India and China — make any substantial debt relief for a category as wide as "middle income countries" a near impossibility in the current political climate. Further, the definition excludes small island states that are categorised as "high income," such as Antigua and Barbuda, The Bahamas, Barbados, Seychelles, Singapore, and Saint Kitts and Nevis. Some of these so-called "high-income" states, as mentioned before, are currently constrained by large debt burdens that demand structured relief.

Before Jamaica settled on advocacy for a HIMIC initiative, it was interested in "a special category of Small Vulnerable and Highly Indebted Middle Income countries".[26] Such a formulation had the benefit of being more narrowly-focussed, though it still excluded "high income" islands through its implicit endorsement of the inapplicable metric of per capita GDP as a means of categorising island states. As such, both formulations, while worthy of support, are insufficiently island-specific. The debt profiles of high-income Antigua and Barbuda and the Seychelles have more in common with middle-income islands such as Grenada or Cape Verde than they do with their fellow high-income states like Germany, South Korea or the United States. Indeed, the debt incurred by Small Island Developing States — which is invariably rooted in issues related to small populations, small economies, over-reliance on a few sectors like tourism or primary commodities, and costs related to disaster recovery or climate adaptation — have far more in common with each other than they do with large, well-popu-lated, non-island nations. Similarly, the type and scope of debt relief instruments — such as debt for climate swaps,[27] hurricane clauses[28] or various other policy commitments that could be made in exchange for such relief — are more likely to have coherence and uniform appli-cability if confined to the island context. Whatever the acronym cho-sen (for example, VIDA — Vulnerable Island Debt Alleviation) Small Island States must coalesce around advocacy for debt relief based on the common specificities of smallness, islandness and vulnerability.

In addition to island-specific debt relief, there are three addition-al adjustments to lending and debt-calculation practices that are nec-essary in this new reality of increased vulnerability for small island states. First, all vulnerable Small Island Developing States should have equal access to concessionary lending from multilateral insti-tutions. In per capita terms, The Bahamas ranks among the richest countries in the world, based on its population of fewer than 400,000 people. However, its *total* GDP of only US $12 billion ranks it in the bottom third of the independent countries of the world. The 700 low-lying islands in The Bahamas' archipelago will not be made resilient by averages. It will take actual money. Their adaptation will require far greater resources than The Bahamas can credibly gener-ate or borrow on non-concessionary terms.

Second, to the extent that Bretton Woods Institutions continue to use rough debt ratios as a basis to diagnose and prescribe, those data must be properly contextualised. Debt related to infrastructure spending and certain developmental investments should be distin-guished from current consumption and either excluded from debt-to-GDP calculations or otherwise distinguished for analytical purposes. In this era of high-tech data gathering and enhanced analysis, it is incredible that such crude and outmoded metrics continue to have a profound impact on countries' developmental paths.

Third, islands are not merely powerless victims of the Bretton Woods system. They must invest focussed, high-level political muscle into reforming the institutions, particularly regarding voice, vote and quota allocations, to ensure that islands and their allies have stronger voices and influence in improving the conditions of island engagement.

In the current economic context, debt doesn't mean what it used to, particularly for small island developing states. However, as a limitation on valuable fiscal space and as an inhibitor of urgent investments in development and climate resilience, debt relief and restructuring must play a central role in any serious international commitment to our shared sustainable development objectives.

CHAPTER TWO

Aid, Trade and Trading Aid

Nah Beg Dem Nuttin'

- Elephant Man

The patience and forbearance of the poor are among the strongest bulwarks of the rich.[29]

- C.L.R. James

In 2008, Bruce Golding — then the Prime Minister of Jamaica — detonated a diplomatic bomb within the Caribbean Community when he caricatured unnamed Caribbean leaders as global mendicants, accusing them of "go[ing] around, hat in hand, to every capital of the world like panhandlers on the street, telling people how we are like the wretched of the earth; we are poor and that we need all sorts of charity. I am tired of that . . . Not only am I tired of it, but I believe that we have allowed it to cause us to put off indefinitely the need to confront some of our own weaknesses and deficiencies and to deal with them." Golding's broadside against aid and the pursuit of international cooperation sat awkwardly and incongruously with his simultaneous "call on the international community to devise strategic programmes to address the peculiar needs of middle income countries with deep pockets of poverty. Because of these factors and our exposure to frequent natural disasters, Jamaica and its CARICOM partners are proposing the international recognition of CARICOM states as a special category of Small Vulnerable and Highly Indebted Middle Income countries."[30] The legacy of Golding's bracing call for economic self-sufficiency was further sullied by his own hat-in-hand genuflection before the International Monetary Fund less than two years later, in exchange for a US $1.27 billion IMF programme that was designed to "generate about US $1.1 billion in [additional] funding from other international financial institutions".[31] That 2010 programme begat a second US $932 million Extended Fund Facility from the IMF in 2013, which in turn led to a further US $1.7 billion Stand-By-Arrangement in 2016. Jamaican editorial writers are already suggesting that a further IMF programme may be necessary in 2019.[32]

Nonetheless, despite Golding's reality check, donor countries have entrenched a global mythology of the Protestant Work Ethic that manages to stigmatise "aid" as a shameful and self-perpetuating form of international welfare. This stereotype is often reinforced by opportunistic politicians in recipient countries, without references to local constraints, global imbalances, and the abject failure of almost all developed countries to meet their longstanding commitment to provide 0.7% of their gross national product for Official Development Assistance.[33] Various euphemisms, from "aid sustainability" to "aid effectiveness" to "Aid for Trade" to "graduation" from aid eligibility, have arisen to buttress the underlying conventional narrative that development assistance is an undeserved and unsustainable form of international charity, given to States that have failed to take advantage of abundant available opportunities to achieve prosperity through the global trade in goods and services.

In the context of Small Island States, this is a false narrative.

The truth is that Small Island Developing States have, by and large, achieved remarkable levels of development in a relatively short period of post-independence development. The fact is that, this development has been achieved despite historical exploitation, neocolonial manipulation and coordinated economic marginalisation that has banished most Small Island Developing States to the outermost peripheries of the global financial system. The reality is that the overwhelming majority of macroeconomic and existential challenges facing island states — from global economic crises to commodity price fluctuations to climate change — originate well beyond island shores and instead have their genesis in the capitals of large states most likely to feign donor fatigue or climate denial. As recipients of development assistance, most Small Island Developing States are in actuality well-governed, have comparatively low levels of official corruption, and possess strong records of effectively applying development assistance — a record that would be stronger but for the labyrinthine and burdensome bureaucratic processes demanded by donors with a one-size-fits-all approach to aid disbursement. Nonetheless, the overriding and inescapable fact is that every single independent Small Island Developing State requires development assistance to meet the current externally-imposed challenges of iniquitous globalisation, economic crises and climate change.

Myths of "Aid for Trade" & "Rules-based Trade"

Almost two decades ago, the international community appeared to commit to the notion that developing states could achieve prosperity through increased global trade in goods and services. In 2001, amid much fanfare, the World Trade Organisation (WTO) launched the "Doha Development Round" in Qatar, promising to secure for developing states "a share in the growth of world trade commensurate with the needs of their economic development".[34] In a masterpiece of ambiguous diplomatic non-committal commitment, the Doha Declaration also stated:

> *We agree to a work programme, under the auspices of the General Council, to examine issues relating to the trade of small economies. The objective of this work is to frame responses to the trade-related issues identified for the fuller integration of small, vulnerable economies into the multilateral trading system, and not to create a subcategory of WTO Members. The General Council shall review the work programme and make recommendations for action to the Fifth Session of the Ministerial Conference.*[35]

That Fifth Session of the Ministerial Conference, concluded in 2003, movingly attempted to "reaffirm our commitment to the Work Programme on Small Economies"[36] and "take note" of more substantive recommendations, while deferring any substantive action on the role of small economies in the global financial system. The can continued to be kicked down the road, up to the collapse of the trade negotiations in 2008.

A purported innovation of the Doha talks was the concept of "Aid for Trade". The Aid for Trade agenda was designed to mobilise resources to address the trade-related constraints in developing countries. As a concept, Aid for Trade was widely accepted and endorsed, partly because it reinforced two ideological, as opposed to economic, biases. First, it entrenched the notion that developing countries simply required a small push to integrate more fully into casino capitalism, and once integrated, they would achieve a type of prosperity that would free donor countries from their historical obligations. Second, "Aid for Trade," like "Welfare to Work," is one of those glib catchphrases that sounds eminently logical, but masks the underlying puritanical bias that one must not get "something for nothing," or should be taught to fish instead of simply given one. However, enthusiasm for the Aid for Trade concept never translated into sufficient resources to achieve its stated objectives, beyond a few isolated sectoral successes in a limited number of countries. Certainly, no island state has so benefited from Aid for Trade as to make further aid unnecessary or to place island economies in the mainstream of global trade.

Indeed, in the context of Small Island Developing States, Aid for Trade's tinkering with supply-side constraints may be welcome, but cannot address the structural island-specific challenges that impede effective global trade: small size, limited productive base, high costs of inputs, transportation costs, and most importantly, the WTO's own rules that were weaponised to destroy the banana export trade and limit the policy tools available to protect and grow local businesses. Aid for Trade is designed to address internal trade-related obstacles, but when the obstacles are in-built, external or systemic, and when viable opportunities in targeted, emerging niches are ignored, Aid for Trade is little more than a slogan.

Small island states exist in a reality where the Doha Development Round has imploded, and with it the possibilities of beneficial trade arrangements for economies on the global periphery. The world's largest economies are demonstrably uninterested in multilateral trade agreements or any adjustments to the current system that pose even the slightest potential to upend the current economic order. Instead, those large economies engage in bilateral trade wars and fuel protectionist trends that further limit the small states' options to engage in meaningful global trade. These failures to complete development-centred adjustments to the trade apparatus, to restrain large state excesses and to remain within the confines of a rules-based multilateral system further buttress the perception that the trading system is rigged against the legitimate interests of small island developing states.

The WTO cases involving bananas and online gambling illustrate the perils of being a small state in a large system that is indifferent to the point of hostility.

The infamous Banana Trade Wars began in 1993, when the European Union set quotas favouring banana imports from the small islands of the Caribbean and the Pacific, as well as some African nations. The EU viewed the quotas as necessary to facilitate trade and address the developmental needs of the states that had been victims of European colonialism, as well as pursue the EU's broader trade and development objectives. However, the United States, on behalf of American multinational banana producers in Latin America, challenged the quota arrangement before the WTO. The interests of the United States — a country that did not export a single banana, and whose multinationals did not employ American workers — trumped those of the European banana importers and the small island states whose entire economies were based on banana export. When the EU finally capitulated to the WTO in 2009, the then-European Commission president, José Manuel Barroso, hailed the resolution as "a compromise that works for all sides," and "an important boost for the multilateral system".[37] Small island states would beg to differ. In Saint Vincent and the Grenadines, for example, the value of quota-era banana exports to Europe amounted to as much as one fifth of its GDP. Today, that number is zero.

The effort to restructure post-banana island economies, on the fly, has been arduous. In purportedly applying the rules in defence of free trade, rather than in the interest of individual states, the WTO chose to decimate small island economies rather than adopt the equally valid option of permitting *de minimis* commerce that did no violence to the global trading system.

Unfortunately, the case of Antigua and Barbuda's challenge to the United States' "Measures Affecting the Cross-Border Supply of Gambling and Betting Services"[38] illustrates that even when small states prevail legally, they have few options to enforce their judgments against large powers that simply choose to ignore the rules. In 2003, Antigua and Barbuda filed suit in the WTO after American special interest groups encouraged their government to prosecute foreign-based suppliers of online gambling services and legislatively hobble the Antiguan online gaming industry. The WTO ruled in favour of Antigua and Barbuda. The United States, however, has effectively ignored the ruling and failed to bring its legislation in compliance with the applicable provisions of the General Agreement on Trade in Services — a bedrock treaty in the architecture of global trade. Faced with this American non-compliance, the WTO authorised Antigua and Barbuda to suspend US $21 million annually in intellectual property rights held by U.S. firms. In other words, Antigua and Barbuda was given the legal right to "pirate" millions of dollars worth of movies, music, books, software, inventions and patented designs. However, the United States has also ignored this award, content to call Antigua and Barbuda's bluff that a small island state would not seek to antagonise the mighty United States over such a relatively paltry sum. Even when Antigua and Barbuda was walloped by a massive hurricane, and they pleaded with the United States to settle its WTO judgment to fund post-disaster reconstruction,[39] the American government ignored the request.

The lesson to be gleaned from these two unfortunate experiences of small island states before the WTO is not simply that the United States always gets its way. Instead, it is evidence of the ways in which inequality and small state prejudice are hard-wired into the existing economic order. At best, it relegates developing countries to tactical rather than strategic players in the international trade regime.[40]

However, Small Island Developing States have neither the power to ignore nor enforce rulings of global economic arbiters. At the margins, therefore, the rules of the economic game can only exist to the detriment of small island states. The collapse of the Doha Development Round laid bare the fundamental failure of the developed and developing countries of the world to agree on a shared social purpose[41] or common understanding of the role of multilateral trade in achieving development. Nowhere are the manifestations or effects of seemingly-unbridgeable ideological chasm more apparent than in the case of small island states.

The prospects for new or innovative forays into trade by Small Island Developing States are thwarted at every turn by either the rules of powerful bodies or the whims of powerful players. In 2011, Jamaican economist Norman Girvan decried the "fiscal colonialism" of the Organisation for Economic Co-operation and Development (OECD), for its attempts to eliminate the international financial services sector in Caribbean countries; and the "economic colonialism" of the European Union, which forced those same countries into a one-sided Economic Partnership Agreement (EPA) that forces them to commit to a harmful form of liberalisation with little practical developmental advantage for small islands.[42] Today, the fiscal and economic colonialism described by Girvan is even more pronounced. In 2018, the OECD and the European Union strong-armed Caribbean countries into adopting suicidal legislation that will cripple, if not destroy, the financial services sector in many island economies. The EPA forced down the throat of Caribbean countries has yet to produce any significant economic benefit to Caribbean business or industry. Its sole success was in avoiding the wrath of the European Union.

Faced with the WTO's destruction of the banana industry, the European Union's decimation of the financial services sector, and the EPA's sacrifice of local markets for the ephemeral promise of European market access, the developmental impact of meaningful international trade has been less far less than advertised. The sovereign decision by some islands to sell citizenship and passports as their only remaining commodity worth trading — however objectionable and mercenary — is now facing the familiar international regulatory noose-tightening that besets all island economic initiatives beyond tourism and small-scale agriculture.

Developmental options are limited for states on the fringes of a neoliberal economic order — particularly those with in-built constraints and vulnerabilities. At this stage of islands' developmental journey, there are few, if any, small island states that do not require grants, concessional loans, debt relief, or knowledge transfers from bilateral or multilateral sources. However, this need for aid is often stymied by an insufficient commitment by donor countries and enduring stereotypes about which nations are more deserving of aid or less likely to squander it.

Development Assistance: Too Little, Too Late

In 1970, at the dawn of the so-called "Second United Nations Development Decade," the international community resolved that:

> *Each economically advanced country should endeavour to provide by 1972 annually to developing countries financial resource transfers of a minimum net amount of 1 per cent of its gross national product at market prices in terms of actual disbursements…. Those developed countries which are unable to achieve this target by 1972 will endeavour to attain it not later than 1975.*

> *In recognition of the special importance of the role which can be fulfilled only by official development assistance, a major part of financial resource transfers to the developing countries should be provided in the form of official development assistance. Each economically advanced country will progressively increase its official development assistance to the developing countries and will exert its best efforts to reach a minimum net amount of 0.7 per cent of its gross national product at market prices by the middle of the Decade.*[43]

The target of providing 0.7% of GNP was first proposed in 1969 by the influential *Partners in Development: Report of the Commission on International Development*,[44] dubbed the "Pearson Report" in recognition of former Canadian Prime Minister Lester B. Pearson, who helmed the Commission on International Development at the behest of then-World Bank President Robert McNamara. British Prime Minister Harold Wilson said at the time that "I am convinced that [the Pearson Report] will become one of the most important documents of the twentieth century." The *Pearson Report* called for the 0.7% target to be achieved "by 1975 and in no case later than 1980".

Almost forty years after the 1980 deadline, the 0.7% target remains woefully unmet, despite its repeated reiteration in numerous international agreements, from the 2001 Monterrey Consensus, to the 2005 World Summit[45], to the 2005 G8 Gleneagles Summit, to the 2009 Conference on the World Financial and Economic Crisis and Its Impact on Development[46], to the 2015 Addis Ababa Action Agenda[47], and so on. In 2005, the European Union committed to achieving the target by 2015, a position endorsed by the Organisation for Economic Co-operation and Development (OECD). However, on the 50th anniversary of the *Pearson Report*'s recommendation, only five of the OECD's 29 donor countries have managed to achieve the 0.7% target. In fact, the average development assistance commitment in 2017 was a mere 0.31% of developed countries' GNI[48] — less than half of the decades-old target. This failure is even more lamentable in the face of the exponentially increased developmental burdens imposed by climate change adaptation and disaster recovery — burdens imposed largely by the same developed nations that have yet to meet their oft-stated, oft-ignored assistance targets.

Other increased global commitments to development in the post-*Pearson Report* world — most notably the Millennium Development Goals and their successor Sustainable Development Goals — internationally-agreed frameworks that carry with them multi-trillion-dollar price tags. Indeed, implementing the Sustainable Development Goals will cost between US $1.4 trillion and US $6 trillion annually.[49] Even the most conservative estimates, employing the most optimistic projections of economic growth and private sector investment, calculate that there is an annual financing gap of US $152-$163 billion that must be closed by development assistance if Sustainable Development Goals are to be met[50]. Nevertheless, notwithstanding these ever more ambitious international goals and targets, development assistance has plateaued at a level far below long-standing commitments, despite increasingly creative accounting sleight of hand designed to shoehorn all sorts of unrelated expenditure into the "aid" column.

In this light, the regularly-cited malaise of "donor fatigue" is most often a misdiagnosis informed by a donor-centric development perspective. More accurately, developing nations suffer from "commitment fatigue," where all manner of grand pronouncements are endlessly rehashed but seldom honoured. The yawning credibility gap between pledged and delivered development assistance is leading to a cynicism that development assistance is more reliably secured through methods that are non-needs based.

The Aid Trade

There is, of course, a brisk trade in aid, unmoored from any needs-based assessment. This aid is traded between donors and geostrategic recipients, whose location, population or political persuasion merit special great power inducement. Islands, in the past, have not been above the occasional diplomatic decision that is most credibly explained within this framework. However, islands are increasingly located in zones of peace, far away from global hotspots. With the decline of the Soviet Union, and the comparatively chummy relations between the United States and China, thee is no great power rivalry that is sufficiently intense for islands to consistently trade aid as a developmental strategy. Additionally, as development assistance migrates increasingly to bureaucratised multilateral institutions, the scope for meaningful geostrategic windfalls becomes more remote and episodic.

As islands' diplomacies have adapted to modern realities, they have discovered a greater diplomatic value in concerted, coordinated advocacy on matters of importance to islands, and of burnishing their "brand" as principled, responsible actors on the world stage. The trade in aid, though not extinct, is definitely overstated in the island context, and informed by the cynical biases of outside observers.

Pledges, Responsibilities & Obligations

Let us state the obvious: here is "strong evidence that the benefits of globalisation have been polarised in favour of the rich".[51] These benefits are a systemic feature of our current economic architecture, not mere happenstance. To quote U.S. President Donald Trump's diagnosis in a different context: "the system is rigged."

Development assistance is therefore a compensatory levy on advanced economies to address these built-in inequalities, imbalances and stratification in our deeply flawed version of globalised capitalism. It is an essential part of a socioeconomic safety net, designed not to rescue individual countries, but to ensure the perpetuation and stability of the global system itself. Without it, the billions of people who live beyond the borders of advanced economies will begin to ask hard questions about the unchanging predictability of the developmental winners and losers within the existing economic apparatus. Unfortunately, development assistance functions neither as a progressive tax nor a legally enforceable obligation. It is subject to the whims of individual nations and the pendulum of isolationist versus globalist sentiment within the electorates of advanced economies.

Among Small Island Developing States, the lack of predictability of automaticity of development assistance, the often insurmountable bureaucratic hurdles to access, and the inappropriate arbitrariness of the qualifications and barriers to aid, have acute developmental implications. Oftentimes, the small tax base and high debt burden of small island states means that their entire capital budget is funded by development assistance of some sort. Within the framework of a rules-based global trading apparatus that fails to effectively accommodate small economies and continues to constrain the trade in the limited set of goods and services where island states have an advantage, development assistance plays an outsized role.

Within the confines of the existing iniquitous system, small island states must fight both to maximise their space to trade and to secure assistance and cooperation commensurate with their mounting developmental and climate resilience needs. This means a unified front and aggressive advocacy to secure concessions, carve-outs and accommodations — including through brass knuckled diplomatic *realpolitik* at multilateral fora where our voting bloc is under-utilised. The Golding-style mantra of individual island self-reliance, that criticises the aid recipient but not the systems and circumstances that make aid necessary, is of greater utility as a populist political rallying cry than it is as a developmental strategy or critique. Instead, strategies for trade, aid and the diplomatic aid trade require savvy coordinated actions to protect markets and industries, and to guarantee a steady and reliable stream of development assistance tailored to islands' needs and priorities.

CHAPTER THREE

The Quest for a Niche

All we have is just sea water and sand

- The Mighty Chalkdust

By the sweat of thy brow shalt thou eat bread.

- Holy Bible, Genesis 3:19

There is no playbook for small island development, no proven set of prescriptions or successful precedents from which a developmental roadmap could be discerned. The dominant view among mainstream development economists is that "small states are no different from large states, and so should receive the same policy advice that large states do,"[52] a position largely endorsed by the one-size-fits-all development programmes traditionally administered by the Bretton Woods Institutions. Others suggest, either disdainfully or dispassionately, that small island states are "dignified mendicants" on the "pampered periphery" of the world economy, and that their survival is linked to their continued global rentier status, subsisting on one subsidy after another.[53]

While either extreme may represent workable formulae for short-term survival, neither operates as a reliable guide to sustainable development. Both perspectives also suffer from variants of cynical large state bias — either in suggesting that, if its good enough for us big guys, its good enough for you Lilliputs; or in meekly accepting large states' systemic dominance so unquestioningly that it becomes difficult to imagine small states as anything other than a tick on dog's back.

Further, the manufacturing-based, export-led, growth strategies that work for large economies soon run into the size and capacity constraints of small islands, or the moderately successful nations soon achieve per-capita GDP graduation from their "dignified mendicancy". At that point, the limitations of those models as subsistence — as opposed to sustainable — development paradigms become apparent.

From Loophole to Niche

The short history of independent island states has demonstrated their uncanny ability to survive in an unfavourable global environment that lurches from indifference to focussed hostility. Disadvantaged in trade by both inequitable rules and their own structural limitations, small island states have sought opportunities by wedging themselves into the tiniest cracks and fissures of globalisation's edifice — surviving in the loopholes and lacunas of the international order, seeking economic rents for the rendering of inchoate services. If an island is small enough, jumping through loopholes, combined with a corresponding pursuit of development assistance, can prove profitable in the short term:

> *Many microstates today survive and even thrive on a 'rentier status' in the world economy. Rents are revenues which are cut off from any directly productive activity on the part of the recipient: they include aid, remittances from abroad, dividends on foreign securities, licences, stamp duties, customs receipts, land or fishing taxes, leases, loans and payments for the provision of various services — tourism, banking, tax havens, finance, military bases, casinos, yacht berths, space tracking facilities, transshipment, flags of convenience, bunkering, waste dumping sites, philately and other collectors' items — which are collectively known as invisible receipts. Ricardo's aversion to rentiers and Marx's predilection for productive over unproductive labour may both be responsible for the fact that such a survival strategy is looked on as anathema. It is frowned upon as parasitic, fragile and non-entrepreneurial.*[54]

Today, we could add the sale of passports to this list of unproductive rents. However, the inherent fragility of a life among the loopholes is increasing. Far from the permissive neglect of the past that allowed the smallest states to eke out a living in these marginal activities, today's superintendents of globalisation's architecture are closing the loopholes and filling the cracks with renewed zeal. From ship rider agreements to tax haven blacklists to extraterritorial assaults on gambling, banking and citizenship by investment programmes, once profitable loopholes are becoming inexorably tightening developmental nooses. While subsidies decrease, protectionist preferences erode, and developmental assistance stagnates, the energy and creativity required to find the next big loophole is reaching the point of diminishing returns. This pattern is best described as

...a scramble to exploit one niche or opportunity, then another, moving as nimbly as possible from one to the next, or from one crisis to the next, as one dries up and (hopefully) another presents itself. There [is] no elegant progression, no evolution of economic capacity, no macro-level diversification, no hoped-for economic viability, as may have been envisaged by industrialisation-led development models.[55]

Further, local populations weaned on rentier revenues and trained to service ephemeral activities, often find themselves — post loophole closure — with high levels of expectations and contrastingly low levels of transferable productive skills. "With each (often dramatic) ebb of a specific leading sector and the emergence of another, the socio-economy suffers painful dislocation: unemployment and relative poverty set in amongst the losers."[56] Inevitably, boom-and-bust economic oscillations are amplified, and islands endlessly repeat the same developmental dance of one step forward, one step back.

The steadier, more sustainable approach may be to seek out productive, emerging niches in locally-produced goods, services and skills. Unlike loopholes and rentier opportunities, productive niches are rooted in islands' local economy, and cannot be arbitrarily eliminated by the stroke of a distant bureaucrat's pen. Less dependent on the blessing or benign neglect of foreign governments, niche-centred development saves diplomatic and legislative resources for activities other than alternately fighting and complying with overseas rule makers.

There is no shortage of niche opportunities in the global economy. Increasingly discerning travellers demand tailored niche services focussed on yachting, diving, entertainment, cultural, sports, medical, or ecotourism. Opportunities for high-end, well-branded, light manufacturing or niche agricultural products abound, as do potential uses for crops with medicinal value, from marijuana to moringa. With large exclusive economic zones, island states can seek ways to sustainably exploit marine resources themselves, rather than cheaply lease their seascape to foreign extractors. Increasingly affluent Diaspora communities are potential pre-existing niche markets in major metropolitan centres. Labour can be trained for export, as many islands have done with medical professionals, teachers and agricultural workers. Information technology is an underused developmental accelerant, attractor of foreign direct investment, and creator of jobs and knowledge. Islands can also leverage well-educated populations, moderately low wages, proximity to major economies, and participation in regional integrated markets to attract and grow medium-sized businesses.

And so on.

However, there are challenges in de-emphasising traditional economic drivers and placing greater focus on locally-sourced niche products, clever corporate branding, and narrowly-targeted specialised goods and services that compete, not on price, but on other qualitative differentiations. First, the resistance to change cannot be underestimated. With the exception of the comprehensive economic reordering periodically foisted upon them by colonial powers and globalisation's oligarchs, the socio-political culture of island states has tended to be resistant to radical changes. Investing resources in branding and niche production is inherently risky, and there are no reliable means of determining up front whether such an approach will produce sufficient "winners" to offset the decline in rentier revenue. For every Barbados Mount Gay Rum, or Jamaica Blue Mountain

Coffee or Fiji Water are hundreds of products and services that have failed or made negligible impact on state revenues. Change would not be easy.

Second, and more fundamentally, few small island cultures and educational systems are geared towards fostering the type of entrepreneurial innovation that could dependably carry the brunt of a country's developmental aspirations. While it is often difficult to point to direct, causal connections between entrepreneurship and growth in developing countries, there is little doubt that entrepreneurs play essential roles in driving the structural transformation from a traditional to a modern economy.[57] Unfortunately, too many island educational systems are rooted in replicating some bygone facsimile of colonial instruction and fostering a culture where entrepreneurial failure is stigmatised, and youth are groomed to expect lifelong jobs in a bloated public service.

Any sustainable transition towards greater focus on niche-targeted entrepreneurial growth must necessarily invest in an innovation-focused education and economic system that does not mimic other countries, but concentrates on entrepreneurship and training for in-demand skills. Fortunately, it is far easier to retool an island state's small, young population than the large, ageing ones in other states. Such reforms to curriculum, pedagogy and training are well within most islands' capacity. However, the redistributive investments required to improve educational access and deepen the pool of qualified teachers may be more challenging.

To be sure, no internal educational and economic realignment can take place overnight. Any such reconfiguration must also be supported — with time, money, and expertise — by the major core economies whose fingers now hover impatiently on the trigger of islands' economic demise. It is worth recalling that, unlike today's era of instant blacklists and upheaval, the termination of islands' preferential access to banana markets was a protracted affair that allowed time for economic retooling and reinvention. It is also worth noting, however, that European and American development partners encouraged those islands to invest in the financial services sector — the same sector now collapsing under the weight of European and American pursuit of money laundering and tax evasion. Apart from the overall systemic deficiencies that consign small island states to a perilous periphery, globalisation's chief architects and beneficiaries also bear a responsibility for guiding small island states into the very sectors and services they now hope to eliminate. As such, separate and apart from support for development assistance, security and climate reliance, there is a need to allow islands the time, and provide them the adequate resources, to reconfigure their bases of production to a more modern, innovative orientation.

The Road Less Travelled

As such, it is clear that any preference for a shift towards more active pursuit of productive niche entrepreneurship is not informed by some quaint view of self-sufficiency or independence. Nor is it occupied with outmoded value judgments about mendicancy or over-reliance on rentier revenue. Instead, niche-based production and growth is about insulating economic drivers from arbitrary demise, developing a productive population, reducing vulnerability, modulating the wild swings between economic boom and bust, and maximising long-term growth prospects. The increasing stop risks associated with a number of small island states' traditional economic pillars, and the decreasing likelihood that similar pillars are in the offing, necessitate a change in approach. Most island states cannot achieve the scale necessary to compete internationally in the type of standardised, low-value product manufacturing that has driven growth in larger developing economies. Many, too, are approaching a saturation point with tourism services, and a potentially volatile over-reliance on the sector. However, there is ample space to explore the underemphasised developmental path of entrepreneurially pursuing niche markets and branded products, including light manufacturing, that have high value-added potential.

Of course, not all investments in niche entrepreneurship will pay off; and many will be copied or co-opted by foreign capitalist behemoths. But even the failures can add to the knowledge and skills of the population, reveal new opportunities to innovate, and inform the entrepreneurial spirit. In development, as in cricket, you don't have to hit every ball for six to win the game.

CHAPTER FOUR

Inequality and Poverty

Poor people fed up

- Bounty Killer

The basic confrontation which seemed to be colonialism versus anticolonialism, indeed capitalism versus socialism, is already losing its importance. What matters today, the issue which blocks the horizon, is the need for a redistribution of wealth. Humanity will have to address this question, no matter how devastating the consequences may be.[58]

- Frantz Fanon

I n the 1970s, economist Arthur Okun described "the big tradeoff" between equality and economic efficiency.[59] Essentially, Okun's view was that if a country wanted to optimise economic growth, it had to live with the fact that inequality is a by-product of strong capitalist free market competition. Okun's "big trade off" thesis has held sway for the better part of four decades, and relegated inequality data to an interesting footnote to be cited in socialist critiques of the status quo. It was only in the 2010s — and in the context of a very different global economy than the one Okun experienced — that the academic tide began to turn, with a body of work from Daron Acemoglu, Andrew Berg, Samuel Bowles[60], Joseph Stiglitz[61], Jonathan Ostry, and Charalambos Tsangarides[62] arguing forcefully that modern economies require the institutions, innovations, policies, and productivity that come from equitable distribution of wealth, opportunity, capacity and power.

In the small island context, the illogic of inequality has never been open to serious debate. Post-slavery and post-colonial small island societies and economies were textbook examples of inequality: wealth, capacity, education, health, opportunity, means of production and political power were all concentrated in the hands of a privileged few, with vast swaths of rural and racial have-nots relegated to pursuit of a marginal, subsistence existence. In Saint Vincent and the Grenadines, for example, the 1812 census recorded a population of 1,053 whites, 1,482 "coloureds," and 24,920 enslaved Africans. As such, almost all of the country's wealth was concentrated in the hands of the whites, who comprised less than four percent of the population, while 91% of the population owned absolutely nothing — not even their own bodies.

Stripped of preferential colonial trade or welfare arrangements, the unsustainability of this societal makeup became self-evident. The inefficiencies within and beyond the borders of post-colonial island states made survival impossible, to say nothing of even subsistence-level viability. It borders on miraculous that islands have managed to navigate their way out of the deep developmental hole in which they were abandoned by their colonial exploiters.

Unfortunately, that miraculous rise from the ashes of genocide, slavery, indentureship, and colonial exploitation have bequeathed a complex legacy of inequality to island states — one whose precise historical and current contours are markedly different from the inequality of other more studied locales. Unreliable and incomplete data indicate that many island states are disproportionately clustered among the world's more unequal societies. Even among the wealthier islands states, seemingly intractable pockets of poverty remain stubbornly immune to the impetus of economic growth.

For small island states, inequality is a particularly insidious drain on resources and growth. Consider the population of a small island economy — already minuscule — and then consider those who live in poverty, those who lack employable skills, those who receive substandard health care, and those who have neither education, opportunity nor hope. The productive potential and capacity of that tiny island population is further reduced by the tangible costs of inequality. For islands, whose capacity constraints cannot afford any inefficiencies in the use of its human resources, inequality is a mortal developmental wound that must be urgently addressed.

Drowning in the Rising Tide

The Reaganesque solution to inequality in the 1980s and 1990s — as local American policy, as imposed developmental prescription, and as global strategy — was to further enrich the already-rich. The idea of "trickle-down" economics was that wealth would flow from the rich down to the poor, and that a "rising tide would lift all ships" to prosperity. This era also buttressed Okun's "big tradeoff" theory with all sorts of social and moral arguments against wealth redistribution — arguments that have calcified into accepted wisdom in the ensuing decades.

Unfortunately, history has proven that a rising tide does not lift all ships. Those that are stuck in the seabed, run aground or take on water are simply swallowed up by the deluge. To torture the metaphor further, those without a ship altogether, and who can't swim, drown. In the context of small island states, many strata of poor, rural, uneducated citizens have been engulfed by the rising tide, while the yachts of the super rich loll idly overhead. For islands, trickle-down economics neither reduces inequality nor sustains growth.

Subsequent study has further challenged the broad notion that economic growth is the cure to inequality, or that redistributive policies are socialist anathema to modern capitalism. Indeed, the current academic consensus is that inequality is actually harmful to growth

> ...because it deprives the poor of the ability to stay healthy and accumulate human capital; generates political and economic instability that reduces investment; and impedes the social consensus required to adjust to shocks and sustain growth... [Further,] there is surprisingly little evidence for the growth-destroying effects of fiscal redistribution at a macroeconomic level. We do find some mixed evidence that very large redistributions may have direct negative effects on growth duration, such that the overall effect — including the positive effect on growth through lower inequality — may be roughly growth-neutral.[63]

In 2018 the Economic Commission for Latin America and the Caribbean (ECLAC) released a report that chronicled the effects of inequality in the region:

> *[S]ocial gaps and lags have a negative impact on productivity, fiscal policy, environmental sustainability and the spread of the knowledge society. In other words, inequality is inefficient and is an impediment to growth, development and sustainability.*
>
> *Lags in capacities, caused by lags in learning and educational trajectories, and by an outdated education that is unable to provide the skills required in a changing production sector, are an obstacle to innovation and the diffusion of technological progress. Undernutrition incurs huge productivity costs and also has repercussions on lifelong health spending, whether privately or publicly funded. Social protection deficits affect capacities and, at the same time, tend to defer and increase costs, meaning that allowing them to accumulate is a bad investment in the medium term. Informal employment places serious constraints on the funding of pension systems, particularly in the light of the ageing of societies.*[64]

Inequality therefore becomes less a necessary side effect of growth and more a massive drag on development. Separate and apart from the moral or political arguments in favour of levelling the playing field and reducing poverty, inequality is a systemic impediment that small island states, in particular cannot afford to ignore.

Mainstreaming Redistribution

Despite focussed attention, poverty in most independent small island states has proven to be a vexing and persistent problem, causing at least one island Prime Minister to muse publicly about the meaning of Jesus' declaration that "the poor you will always have with you".[65] Nonetheless, for islands, the inescapable fact is inequality is both a symptom and a cause of the limited success of previous poverty reduction efforts.

One or two years of economic growth do not produce meaningful reductions in poverty. It is sustained growth that is central to poverty reduction.[66] Similarly, sustained growth, "and whether most citizens see their living standards rising year after year," is a far better measure of economic performance than is GDP.[67] Inequality, however, is the enemy of sustained periods of growth. According to economists Berg and Ostry:

> *(i) increasing the length of growth spells, rather than just getting growth going, is critical to achieving income gains over the long term; and (ii) countries with more equal income distributions tend to have significantly longer growth spells.*[68]

As such, among island states — whose size, structure and constraints already exacerbate economic volatility — it is critical that priority be placed on urgent efforts to address inequality. Not simply for its own sake, but as a sustainable growth and poverty reduction strategy. Further, beyond poverty, there is ample evidence of the role of inequality in negatively impacting health and crime outcomes. Goal 10 of the Sustainable Development Goals, entitled "Reduced Inequalities," enshrines this objective as part of the current international consensus.[69]

The priority focus on accelerated poverty reduction through reduced inequality necessitates a re-examination of the public policy of redistribution. Many island states have engaged in limited land distribution, subsidised housing and expansions of health and educational access. However, more focussed and coordinated redistributive efforts are required — from safety nets to social expenditures.

To get the most bang for the redistributed buck, small island efforts should focus on three broad areas. First, it must address the poor quality of public goods such as security, education, health and the environment, along with the absence of systems of rules to guarantee equal opportunities.[70] Inequality cannot be addressed without increased public investments in health and education. A key determinant of workers' income is the level and quality of education.

Similarly, inequalities in access to education and health irreparably impede innovation and productivity. In archipelagic island states, the challenge of providing access to quality health and education to distant and often underpopulated islands is daunting. The effective use of information technology must therefore become an integral part of these islands' anti-inequality arsenal.

Second, islands must take specific steps to address high unemployment and low wage growth, beyond simply hoping to hit an elusive growth target that will magically expand their economies' absorptive capacity for labour. Among island states, the unemployment rate among the poor and youth is distressingly high and stubbornly intractable. It cannot be wished away. Further, workers rights must be systemically enhanced by enhancing the voice of labour in the workplace, ensuring the occupational safety of workers, and effectively enforcing anti-discrimination laws and procedures.

Third, island states must be willing to get down among the weeds and tailor redistributive social expenditure to specific, often individual circumstances. The benefit of a small population is that the names of the poor or indigent can be ascertained with specificity, and comfortably compiled on a small spreadsheet. A people-centred approach of specific inquiry and intervention must complement islands' macro-level redistributive efforts.

Wealth for All, or Stall

The levels of global inequality are an obscene indictment on our current economic system. According to the *World Inequality Report*, the poorest half of the world's population earns only nine percent of global income. Even with the rapid growth of massive developing countries like China and India, the top richest individuals in the world have captured twice as much growth as the bottom 50% of individuals since 1980.[71] The United States, with less than five percent of the world's population, controls over 25% of its wealth. Within the United States, the income of the richest 1% increased by 169% between 1980 and 2014, and their share of national income doubled, from 10% to 20%.[72] The ultra rich did even better over the same span. The top 0.1% saw their income increase by 281%, and their share of the wealth triple, while the poor continued to languish. To a greater or lesser extent, these results are replicated worldwide. Indeed, in 1970, the richest one per cent of the world's population owned 8% of global wealth. Today, the richest 1% own almost half of global wealth and are on track to own two-thirds by the year 2030. If income distribution more closely resembled the ratio of the late 70s and early 80s, over $1 trillion more would be going to the bottom 80% of the population, increasing their income by almost 25%.

For islands, this inequality is a challenging and large drag on the sustainability of growth and the reductions of poverty.

There is no "big trade-off" between equality and overall economic performance. On the contrary, greater equality complements greater economic performance. There is, therefore, very little economic downside to frontally confronting inequality through focused and systemic redistributive policies — both within and beyond national borders.

John Maynard Keynes once observed that "the outstanding faults of the economic society in which we live are its failure to provide for full employment and its arbitrary and inequitable distribution of wealth and incomes".[73] Time and the entrenchment of an iniquitous form of globalisation have only made Keynes' observation more apt. Among island states, indigenous genocide, slavery and centuries of colonial exploitation have deeply entrenched a culture of inequality that has been bequeathed from one generation to the next. For many islands — less than eight generations removed from slavery and in their fourth or fifth decade of post-colonial independence — the calcification of various strata of inequality cannot be whittled away merely through incremental economic growth. Island development, more than most, is unavoidably tied to meaningful and sustained efforts to reduce inequality.

CHAPTER FIVE

Small Island, Big Government

We nuh want no capitalist...
And we nuh want no big business plan
We nuh want nuh promise from the UN

- Kabaka Pyramid

The behaviour of governments plays as important a role in stimulating or discouraging economic activity as does the behaviour of entrepreneurs, or parents, or scientists, or priests. It is, however, harder to get into perspective because of political prejudice. On the one side are those who distrust individual initiative, and are anxious to magnify the role of government. On the other side are those who distrust governments, and are anxious to magnify the role of individual initiative.... Sensible people do not get involved in arguments about whether economic progress is due to government activity or to individual initiative; they know that it is due to both, and they concern themselves only with asking what is the proper contribution of each.[74]

- Sir Arthur Lewis

M any economists, imported from or educated in distant locales, speak of "the Private Sector" as if it is some type of
wise, beneficent being. In this telling, the private sector is
a vibrant, innovative, omnipresent seraph that provides services most
efficiently, regulates itself most effectively, and generates growth
most abundantly. The mystical powers of this being are thwarted
only by its malevolent antithesis, "the Government," whose ham-fist-
ed interventions and regulations have no long-term public benefit
beyond the Government's own populist pursuit of its own self-sus-
taining manna, the much-derided "votes".

These economists frequently caution the Government to defer at
all times to the wisdom of the Private Sector, and to avoid at all costs
the blunder of inhibiting in any way its inherent dynamism. "Let the
market decide," is a mantra repeated to the point of truism, as is "one
should never crowd out the Private Sector".

However, the truth is that the small island private sector oftentimes bears little resemblance to the beings studied and worshipped
at the Chicago Business School or the London School of Economics.
Our private sectors are thwarted not so much by Government reg-
ulation as tiny local market size, wide-open borders and anti-protec-
tionist international norms that force our small businesses to compete with global behemoths for market share on inherently unequal
terms. Add to that mix a local consumer class whose tastes and aspirations have been shaped by a steady diet of American cable tele-
vision — what William Demas called "the revolution of rising ex-

pectations"[75] — and for whom most material desires are deferred to their annual shopping trip to Miami, their quarterly barrel shipment from their Brooklyn relatives, or their own Amazon.com purchases, shipped conveniently to their homes.

The small island private sectors are also dominated by traditional business families, whose third and fourth generation suckle contentedly at the teat of their fore-parent's fatted calf, and whose social standing is tied up with the stability and collegiality of their business and class connections. Competition and risk-taking are anathema to this old money retail sector, who will guard their niche with far more vigour than they will attempt to expand it.

Potential new and disruptive entrants to this stodgy club are thwarted by the absence of venture capital, a financial sector of foreign banks who see the islands as outposts that exist solely to pad their auto-loan and home mortgage portfolios, a lingering cultural stigmatisation of business failure, and the fact that larger markets and more favourable environments for startups are usually a short plane ride away.

The result is a local private sector that is not simply a scaled-down version of what exists in larger countries. It is one that is risk-averse, less competitive, and dominated by branch offices of foreign conglomerates for whom business and investment decisions are made in distant corporate boardrooms. Monopolies abound, tacit collusion is commonplace, and large swaths of the service landscape lie fallow, because the investment is simply not worth the limited potential return.

Into this void steps the small island government. Itself cash strapped and human resource constrained, it must become the service provider of last resort: importing goods, controlling prices, regulating competition, and in many cases, operating businesses that are critical to a functioning modern economy. Small island governments simply cannot afford to crowd out the Private Sector. However, they are sometimes sucked into the vacuum created by absent private businesses. Despite the historically well-earned stereotypes, islands' state-owned enterprises are increasingly well-run, accountable, and oftentimes, profitable.

Against this backdrop, the knee-jerk antipathy to limited state involvement in islands' commercial sector is misplaced and misinformed. Whatever the wisdom of policies advocating minimalist government in large, advanced economies, that wisdom is lost in translation to the small island context.

The central conceit of those who attempt to shape economic policy in Small Island States is that the lessons applicable to large states are equally valid in small ones. To their mind, the difference between a national economy of 100,000,000 and one of 100,000 is simply a matter of scale. But economic truisms — if they exist — are not infinitely scalable.

The International Monetary Fund, the post-crisis apostle of austerity, has counselled Caribbean finance ministers to adopt drastic small government measures, and applied them with draconian force in the countries that have had the misfortune to require bailout programmes in the wake of the Global Economic and Financial Crisis. This externally applied austerity has been imposed consistently, even in the wake of 2012 and 2013 admissions by the IMF that the mathematical assumptions undergirding their austerity prescriptions were wildly inaccurate. Subsequent IMF admissions — that there is insufficient information on how austerity works in different economic circumstances; or that austerity can have detrimental short-term impacts on debt-to-GDP ratios — have done little to alter the tent pole significance of small government philosophy in modern Caribbean economic thought.

There is an inherent danger of small government austerity in the small island context that exceeds that of similar programmes in richer, larger countries. There is absolutely no empirical or anecdotal evidence to support the untested assumption that the Private Sector will "pick up the slack" created by a shrinking, retreating small island government. It is self-evident that some of the textbook motivators of an active and innovative private sector — strong demand provided by a large market, or energetic competition to fuel innovation and efficiency — are limited to the point of insignificance in many islands. State abdication of an expansive social and economic presence in the name of an idealised notion of "fiscal responsibility" would likely unleash disruptive socio-political forces that are expensive and developmentally disruptive. Most island governments, faced with the clear dichotomy between "balancing the books" and "unbalancing the country" choose social cohesion.[76] Only the Bretton Woods Institutions' bitter and oft-unnecessary medicine of structural adjustment programmes have inexorably moved islands away from their holistic approach to governance.

An Ill-Fitting Strait Jacket

Whatever its relative merits at the time, the IMF's Washington Consensus was never conceptualised as an island-specific policy framework. The imposition of fiscal austerity, trade liberalisation, deregulation, and privatisation of state enterprises were emergency measures meant to combat the Latin American debt crisis of the 1980s. The major players in that debt crisis — Brazil, Mexico and Argentina — had populations at the time of 150 million, 85 million and 35 million, respectively. As such, each of those nations was larger than the combined size of all independent small island states in the world at the time. Their economies bore little to no resemblance to those of the small, opens economies in most island states. Nonetheless, the Washington Consensus was transposed to islands whose own economic travails were more attributable to global downturns than local mismanagement. Those islands were forced to divest themselves of crucial state-owned companies, placing water, electricity, communications, transportation, and health services in the hands of foreign monopolies whose intent was heavily focussed on extraction and not investment. These foreign monopolies were often no more efficient than their state counterparts, but were far less responsive to popular needs and demands. Island governments' involvement in commercial activity — however vital in the individual context — was stamped out as a contravention of neoliberal orthodoxy.

Even as IMF fealty to the strict letter of the Washington Consensus has waned, the doctrine continues to animate all economic programmes administered by the Bretton Woods Institutions.

Further, the antipathy to state involvement in what is conventionally considered the realm of the private sector infects all aspects of development cooperation. For example, although tourism is the most important economic driver in many island economies, rare is the development partner that is willing to facilitate state involvement in the sector — either as a provider or regulator of tourism services. Hotels, tours and attractions are for the Private Sector, islands are told. Allow private sector competition to drive service and quality. The result of this exile of the state from its most vital sector is that prized real estate is given away to foreign companies; governments race to the bottom in a regional competition to lure private organisations with ever-more-generous concessions; locals employed in the sector are perpetually cursed to being the proverbial hewers of wood and drawers of water,[77] while top-paying, upwardly mobile positions are reserved for foreigners; island governments retain a relatively minuscule proportion of total tourist expenditure; and locals are denied access to the coasts, mountains and rivers that define them as islanders.

Similarly, state involvement in the provision of public goods — from regional air transport to tertiary eduction — is discouraged and subjected to pure "market forces" that subvert the long-term developmental objectives. Conversely, the deification of the Private Sector leads to promotion of the misleadingly-titled "Public Private Partnership," which is fast evolving away from its original intent to mean an arrangement where the state assumes a disproportionate amount of investment risk; guarantees investor profit; subsidises private sector inefficiencies; and is rewarded merely with the positive imprimatur of Private Sector involvement and management.

Prudence and Enterprise

A series of recent publications, from Mark Blythe's *"Austerity: The History of a Dangerous Idea"*[78] to Mariana Mazzucato's *"The Entrepreneurial State: Debunking Public vs. Private Sector Myths"*[79] have punched holes in the myth that austerity is sound developmental policy or that the private sector can innovate effectively in the absence of state support. Nonetheless, these authors have, to date, done little to influence decades of conventional wisdom in support of small governments and unfettered private sectors.

In the small island context, the proven and pragmatic role of the state has been to pursue a path of prudence and enterprise[80]: avoiding fiscal profligacy while maintaining social protections and seeking targeted opportunities to stimulate economic growth — including through participation in private sector activities, if necessary. In eschewing the formalistic application of Washington Consensus Doctrine, this practical approach is the cornerstone of an island-specific engagement with citizens and the private sector in the efficient delivery of goods and services.

The private sector of the smallest island states bears little resemblance to that of larger, more developed economies. Because of the small size and openness of island economies, their trade dependence on a few large partners, and their susceptibility to external shocks, investor confidence is far more dependent on the decisions and health of foreign economies than it is on local circumstances. In reality, small island governments have neither the means nor the inclination to crowd out the Private Sector, and participate only reluctantly in spheres more commonly dominated by private interests. Increased connectivity and affordability of freight means that consumer goods are increasingly procured beyond the shores of island states and shipped inwards, either from online retailers or as goods-based remittances. With tastes long shaped by developed country advertising, the increased accessibility of those goods to islanders, particularly the middle class, means that American online retailers are doing more to crowd out the local private sector than any state action. Increasingly, the small island private sector, like the small islands themselves, must seek niches in the underserved cracks in globalisation's edifice and cede other pursuits to large foreign entities. Similarly, like their public sector partners, the vulnerability of small island private sectors requires expanded support and interaction with governments in a variety of fora. The caricature of the small island government as an innovation-thwarting bogeyman is misplaced and unfounded in the modern context.

Ask most small island Private Sector operators what they want to grow their business and the answer will be more government, not less; more concessions, more loans and subsidies, more infrastructure, more protection from foreign competition, and better public goods. The challenges faced by small island businesses come not from their governments, but from an increasingly borderless trading environment and improved global logistics that put local businesses in increasingly direct competition with global conglomerates.

What does this mean for small island states and their partners in the private sector? It means that while the indispensable role of the private sector in national growth and development is undiminished, the policy tools to facilitate effective private sector enlargement must be deployed within the context of uniquely island realities. The government must continue to facilitate private sector growth. However, the realities of island development mean that their governments can neither be as small or as pure as the textbooks demand. Island governments must be both developmental and entrepreneurial. As such, island governments must recognise those situations in which citizen demands or developmental objectives require creative involvement beyond the typical public sector activities. Similarly, development partners must confront the evidence that globalisation has shaped island private sectors in ways that make them immune to conventional prescription or prediction.

Sometimes, the island government simply has to help run the shop.

CHAPTER SIX

The Climate Threat

Many more will have to suffer
Many more will have to die
Don't ask me why

- Bob Marley

The squandering of oil and gas is associated with one of the greatest tragedies, not in the least resolved, which is suffered by humankind: climate change.[81]

- Fidel Castro

There are thousands of books and academic journals, well-sourced and peer-reviewed, that chronicle the causes of climate change and that model its future impact. There are tens of thousands of reports from climate affected locales with touching stories of death and destruction, or bracing economic data about losses, damage and adaptation costs. There are hundreds of hours of speeches by political leaders, alternately pleading or promising cutbacks, commitments and cooperation. And there are millions of dollars pledged to combat climate change or estimated to address its impacts.

Yet the climate continues to change, the threat continues to grow, and small islands continue to face an uncertain, potentially apocalyptic, future.

It is difficult to imagine a global issue upon which more words have been expended, to produce comparatively few meaningful results, as Climate Change. Small Island Developing States have talked themselves hoarse over the years in various efforts to raise the alarm, put a human face on what was an esoteric scientific debate, and push multilateral negotiations towards a conclusion that would save lives and safeguard the very existence of nations.

Today, islands continue to raise their voices to encourage urgent action on climate change. But those voices are now tinged with frustration and anger as the toll of death and destruction continues to increase; as climate events grow more frequent and severe with each passing year; and as the window of opportunity for decisive action shrinks rapidly.

Island leaders have grown tired of telling major emitters that climate change is an urgent problem — an existential problem. The defining challenge of our times. The response to islands' alarms has been hollow promises, crocodile tears and studied indifference to the root causes of our distress. To date, the response of major emitters amounts to a reckless and criminal disregard of the consequences and obligations of their actions.

The initial optimism and faith that islands invested in annual negotiating conferences to confront climate change was, at best, naïve and premature. Twenty-four annual Conferences of Parties (COPs) to the United Nations Framework Convention on Climate Change have yielded incremental progress where decisive change was required. Nine years removed from the Copenhagen COP — which was supposed to "seal the deal" on Climate Change — successive Conference hosts have sought to dampen expectations and kick the can down the road towards ever-distant horizons. Despite the intensifying global threat of climate change with its real and ruinous present-day impacts, historical and major emitters continue to act as if the planet has time on its side. The excuses offered for continued inaction — be they political, historical, scientific or economic — grow increasingly indefensible. The prospects of genuine progress against climate change become increasingly remote with each passing day of diplomatic dithering, buck-passing and finger-pointing.

The deepening crisis that is climate change cannot continue to be confronted at the glacial pace of business-as-usual multilateral diplomacy. Round after round of inconclusive global summitry, whatever its intent, has only served to allow major emitters to defer the radical actions that are necessary to restructure and reinvent their economic bases and modes of production. The vacuum created by our multilateral stasis has allowed various countries or blocs to champion unilateral or bilateral initiatives that make headlines but achieve little genuine progress towards the cuts and commitments that are actually required.

1.5 to Stay Alive. . . Over Three, You Cease to Be

Nine years ago, at a Climate Summit in Copenhagen, Denmark, that was advertised as the world's best opportunity to "Seal the Deal" on climate change,[82] a slogan was born:

"1.5 to Stay Alive"

That slogan was coined by the Alliance of Small Island States (AOSIS) to highlight the fact that some small islands will disappear if the average global temperature rises more than 1.5 °C above pre-industrial levels. They will simply be swallowed up by the rising seas. Entire populations will have to be re-settled elsewhere. Entire nations and civilisations will simply cease to exist. The "1.5 to Stay Alive" slogan was meant to highlight the plight of island states, which are more vulnerable to climate change than many larger countries. Climate scientists predict a number of apocalyptic scenarios for planet earth's global temperatures to rise over 2°C above pre-industrial levels; but for many small islands, the short distance between 1.5 and 2°C is the difference between life and death.

In December 2014, Peru hosted the United Nations' 20th climate conference. Those hoping to keep temperature rise below 1.5 °C received a shocking wake-up call. The final declaration for the Peru Conference said:

> *Noting with grave concern the significant gap between the aggregate effect of Parties' mitigation pledges in terms of global annual emissions of greenhouse gases by 2020 and aggregate emission pathways consistent with having a likely chance of holding the increase in global average temperature below 2 °C or 1.5 °C above pre-industrial levels...*[83]

Reading between the diplomatic lines, that paragraph contained a damning condemnation of the process: governments are nowhere close to keeping the temperature rise under 1.5°C. In spite of the steady drumbeat of headline-grabbing pledges from China, India, the USA and the EU that sound great individually, the cumulative weight of those commitments is shockingly inadequate. The planet is much closer to a cataclysmic 4 °C rise over pre-industrial levels than it is to 1.5°. A 4° rise makes the Caribbean unliveable, and guarantees that most Pacific islands vanish from the face of the earth.[84]

This caution is echoed by the Intergovernmental Panel on Climate Change (IPCC) — a global scientific body that analyses "the scientific, technical and socio-economic information relevant to understanding the scientific basis of risk of human-induced climate change, its potential impacts and options for adaptation and mitigation". Their *5th Assessment Report on Climate Change* was published in 2015.[85] The chapters on Small Islands, Coastal Systems and Low-Lying Areas, and Food Security and Food Production Systems are particularly relevant to small island developing states. In summary, here's what the IPCC scientists say is in store for small islands:

- More sea level rise

- More hurricanes

- Changing rainfall patterns — more floods and droughts

- Increases in submergence, coastal flooding and coastal erosion

- Increases in the erosion of beaches, sand dunes and cliffs

- Degrading of fresh groundwater

- Coral bleaching, reef degradation

- Negative impact on fisheries due to destruction of reef ecosystems and migration of fish stocks

- Some islands rendered uninhabitable by sea level rise

- Hundreds of millions of people will be affected by coastal flooding and will be displaced due to land loss by year 2100

- Malaria, dengue, chikungunya, cholera, leptospirosis and other health risks to increase

- Deterioration in standards of sanitation and hygiene due to freshwater scarcity and more intense droughts and storms

- Increase in invasive species and aquatic pathogens

- Greater economic impact in small islands from sea level rise and hurricanes because most of their population and infrastructure are in the coastal zone

- All aspects of food security are affected by climate change, including food access, utilisation and price stability

- Lower crop yields in the Caribbean resulting in lower nutrition quality

- Changes in temperature and precipitation will contribute to increased global food prices by 2050, with estimated increases ranging from 3% to 84%, depending on the crop

- Projected lengthening seasonal dry periods and increasing frequency of drought are expected to increase demand for water throughout the Caribbean

- Caribbean tourism to potentially decline in the medium term by as much as US $146 million

In 2019, the IPCC issued a Special Report called *Global Warming of 1.5°C*, which buttressed these points[86], each of which could merit its own in-depth analysis. A full read of the voluminous IPCC reports makes one thing abundantly clear: islands' very existence hangs in the balance.

Paying for Climate Change

The greatest long-term threat to the development of small islands is climate change. The greatest immediate threat to the development of any individual small island is a natural disaster, caused, quickened or exacerbated by climate change. The grave and gathering menace of climate change is the inescapable, incalculable risk that looms over every forecast, plan or aspiration. Island states are on the verge of being "climatised" out of existence. Unfortunately, the severity of this risk is compounded by the uncertainty surrounding global support for climate change adaptation, and islands' grim realisation that they have been victimised by a cynical diplomatic bait-and-switch on much-needed climate financing.

At the pivotal 2009 Copenhagen Conference, the contours of a grand bargain were defined between the most vulnerable states and those most responsible for their predicament. The developed and wealthy countries placed their most valuable commodity on the table — money — in exchange for the developing world's most precious commodity: their dwindling time to survive. At its most basic, the Copenhagen Accord and subsequent COP outcomes formally enshrined an agreement of buying time. Those who wanted immediate action, gave the developed countries' time — until 2020 — to reform their economic base and reduce their emissions. In return, the developed world pledged money to help mitigate, offset and adapt to the effects of their deferred action. In addition to being an indication of seriousness and good faith, the pledged funding was a monetary down payment on future policy action.

But the deal of dollars for degrees — of buying time — has unravelled, distressingly so. The pledged resources, already inadequate to begin with, are billions of dollars off target and hidden behind labyrinthine access and disbursement procedures. It is a false promise. Unfortunately, islands' time has already been spent. Nine consecutive years of above-average temperature have elapsed. The oceans have warmed and risen. The storms and hurricanes have intensified. The floods have worsened. The droughts have lengthened. Islands cannot turn back the clock, and they have precious little time left to give.

In the realm of adaptation finance, it is necessary to reflect on what was promised, what is being delivered, what is actually needed.

Back in 2009, as the outcome of the Copenhagen Accord hung in the balance, and the United Nations' much-ballyhooed pledge to "seal the deal," teetered on the brink of self-parody, the then-US Secretary of State made a seemingly-bold suggestion: developed countries would pledge US $100 billion per year to help the most vulnerable stave off and prepare for the effects of climate change. Developing countries and island states, without studying the sufficiency of the suggestion, latched on to the pledge as a firm commitment of tangible resources and backed off on their insistence on immediate changes and a hard 1.5°C limit on global warming. A deal was struck.

The Copenhagen Accord committed developed countries "to a goal of mobilising jointly US 100 billion dollars a year by 2020 to address the needs of developing countries".[87] This money, should have a "balanced allocation between adaptation and mitigation". Further, "funding for adaptation will be prioritised for the most vulnerable developing countries, such as the least developed countries, small island developing States and Africa."[88] Subsequent UN climate conference decisions, most notably the 2015 Paris Agreement, reiterated these commitments.[89]

Today, it is clear that the arbitrary US $100 billion pledge will not be met. Even with the most generous accounting, self-reporting and double counting of previously-pledged assistance, the developed world is far off of its commitment. The United Nations' Standing Committee on Finance, in its third *Biennial Assessment of Climate Fi-*

nance, estimates that international public climate finance flows are up to about $58 billion.[90] The Organisation for Economic Co-operation and Development (OECD), in totting-up its own members' commitments, predicts that "developed countries' public finance in 2020 is projected to be close to USD 67 billion (approximately USD 37 billion of bilateral public finance and USD 30 billion of multilateral public finance attributable to these countries),"[91] — $33 billion short of the modest Copenhagen pledge. On the eve of the 2020 deadline, the settled consensus is that the pledge will not be fulfilled.[92]

Worse still, the goal that "[t]he provision of scaled-up financial resources should aim to achieve a balance between adaptation and mitigation"[93] is far off course. Best estimates suggest that only 25% of the financial resources is being targeted to adaptation.[94] This dearth of resources for adaptation is of particular concern to small island developing states for whom adaptation resources are the difference between existence and oblivion.

While the UN climate agreements determined that "significant portion of such [climate] funding should flow through the Copenhagen Green Climate Fund,"[95] roughly 4% of the money is being routed through this facility.[96] This is probably for the best. The Fund's internal administrative problems and labyrinthine access procedures have benefited no one, and developing countries have lost confidence in its ability to deliver meaningful support to their existential struggles.[97]

Tragically, even this "will they or won't they" speculation about whether developed countries will meet their annual $100 billion pledge is beside the point. The pledge — an arbitrary number plucked from the sky in the heat of a political negotiation — is unconnected to what is actually needed to adequately fund adaptation and mitigation. The required level of global adaptation financing alone — which is currently receiving roughly $20 billion annually, at best — is estimated to be between $100 billion and $500 billion by 2050, depending on the extent to which developed countries miss their commitments to curb greenhouse gas emissions. According to a 2010 World Bank report, "the cost between 2010 and 2050 of adapting to an approximately 2° C warmer world by 2050 is in the range of $75 billion to $100 billion a year".[98] However, as has been indicated, global warming is currently projected to overshoot 2° C by a wide margin. A more recent and more realistic estimate by the United Nations Environment Program states that "the annual costs of adaptation could range from US $140 billion to US $300 billion by 2030 and from US $280 billion to US $500 billion by 2050".[99]

These are sobering estimates. For small islands, the upshot is terrifyingly simple: projected global warming and sea level rise will wipe many islands off the map. Projected resources required to adapt to and prevent that annihilation are orders of magnitude more than what is currently being provided.

The Undiplomatic Diplomacy of Climate Change

In that context, it is not hyperbolic to say that the continuing refusal of major polluters to meaningfully mitigate their emissions constitutes an undisguised act of aggression against small island states and their populations. In the face of that aggression, small island states — out-manned and out-gunned in this battle — must coordinate an energetic strategy of asymmetric diplomatic warfare designed to extract concessions, commitments and the resources necessary to fund adaptation efforts.

Despite the failings and inefficiencies of the UNFCCC's intergovernmental process to date, multilateralism is the only mechanism that allows island states a seat at the table and a voice in discussing their own destiny. Over endless rounds of negotiations in those multilateral fora, small island states have bent but not broken in the thus-far futile pursuit of an acceptable solution. The current incrementalism, lack of ambition and multilateral gridlock must be broken in the interest of small states, developing nations, and those countries with a genuine interest in success at solving our climate conundrum.

Success has a clear definition: emissions targets that ensure global temperature increases below 1.5° C, in relation to pre-industrial levels; urgent, predictable, new and easily accessible adaptation financing, whose parameters will be determined not by the comfort of developed countries, but instead by the actual needs of those most affected; a legal basis to penalise the non-compliant.

What this all means is that the diplomatic and advocacy play book must be rewritten. New alliances, new tactics and new arguments are required. 1.5 °C is still the target, but it is becoming less and less of a realistic goal with each passing day. Island states must fight in every venue and at every opportunity for that target, but they must also prepare for the possibility of a world with a temperature increase of two or more degrees. That means more money — much more money — to fund adaptation from those major emitters responsible for climate change. They must realise that either they pay to change their internal modes of production and consumption, or they pay more for the external damage that they cause. While the required resources seem large in absolute dollar terms, the World Bank has pointed out that it is "of the same order of magnitude as the foreign aid that developed countries now give developing countries each year, but it is still a very low percentage of the wealth of countries as measured by their GDP".[100] When one considers that developed countries' Official Development Assistance is currently less than 0.4% of their GDP, providing adaptation financing is not a particularly daunting task.

Island states have arrived at a stand up and fight moment. The public diplomacy and advocacy of the Alliance of Small Island States (AOSIS) has been focused on explaining what will happen to island states if the climate change is not controlled, and hoping that gentle moral suasion would guilt major emitters into action. AOSIS has resisted strong calls from within the group to be a revolutionary — even disruptive — force in climate change negotiations out of concern that such action would marginalise the bloc or be counterproductive to the overall process. But islands cannot be complicit handmaidens to their own destruction. In defence of their right to exist, they must unambiguously and collectively demand that those with the responsibility and the means step up and solve this problem.

Traditional North-South negotiating blocs have, to date, proven inadequate to tackle Climate Change. If the major emitters and fossil fuel producers of the global South are reluctant to recognise the urgency of this moment, new alliances must be formed. Islands must consider legal innovative challenges to those countries and companies scientifically proven to be major climate change contributors. In the absence of enforcement mechanisms in the existing climate accords, islands must fashion their own and make climate compliance the litmus test that guides their diplomatic engagement and alliances. Islands must weigh the cost of derailing the process against the cost of acquiescing to a process that ensures their destruction. If business as usual continues on the climate front, destruction is all but certain.

CHAPTER SEVEN

A Word on Vulnerability

As soon as a hurricane gone,
another one come,
another one a come

- Mr. Vegas

I n November 2018, Brexit Secretary Dominic Raab came under withering scrutiny in the press for realising, apparently belatedly, that the United Kingdom is an island nation.[101] Noting that the UK is a "peculiar geographic, economic entity," Raab highlighted his country's reliance on sea trade, imports, port infrastructure, and the vulnerabilities inherent on that reliance.

Roughly one year before Raab's lesson in geography and economy, United States President Donald Trump experienced his own epiphany. Answering critics of his government's response to the catastrophic devastation wrought by Hurricane Maria in Puerto Rico, Trump took time to explain to the media that "the response and recovery effort probably has never seen something like this. This is an island surrounded by water. Big water. Ocean water."[102]

Lost in the media ridicule on either side of the Atlantic was the fundamental truth being discussed, however inelegantly, by both Raab and Trump: islands are inherently more vulnerable — economically and environmentally — than comparable non-island states, that big ocean water surrounding islands can isolate and inundate. It can raise the costs of trade, communication and disaster recovery. As it warms and rises, it can increase the likelihood of storms and inexorably swallow islands whole, one meter at a time.

Economically, our vulnerability is compounded by a high degree of economic openness, insufficient diversification in production, thin markets, and excessive dependence on a narrow range of exports and strategic imports. The impact of climate events on the economic health of islands can be devastating — from the cost of recovery to the impact that the interruption of production of goods and services can have in an island where few large sectors dominate the economic landscape.

These vulnerabilities contribute to the massive volatility in islands' economic fortunes. The cost of cushioning and building resilience to those vulnerabilities and volatilities often results in accumulations of large debt burdens, as discussed elsewhere in this publication. Islands' status as peripheral and voiceless actors on globalisation's grand stage further subjects their economies to the whims and fancies of distant decision-makers.

Islands' vulnerability to external shocks — both economic and climate-related — pose persistent challenges to their development. Those vulnerabilities, in turn, are increasingly shaping islands from a social, economical, physical, cultural, environmental, and institutional perspective.

While there are some things that islands can and must do to build resilience — from infrastructural investments to integration arrangements to governance and economic reforms — many of their vulnerabilities are in-built. Islands cannot get bigger. They cannot relocate from storm-plagued latitudes. They cannot significantly change their topography. That big ocean water isn't going anywhere. As climate change intensifies, those built-in vulnerabilities only increase.

None of this constitutes a particularly innovative insight.

However, what is striking is the degree to which vulnerability is simply not taken into account when considering the developmental needs of island states. The World Bank, which revels in its role as the global leader in development financing, accepts that islands suffer from greater and more specific vulnerabilities than other states in ways that are not reflected in crude calculations of per capita income.

However, bureaucratic fealty to the status quo has caused them to essentially ignore the issue:

> *In practice, existing vulnerability indices are primarily used for classification or ranking purposes and not for resource allocation. In recent replenishments, [The International Development Association] explored the possibility of using vulnerability metrics as part of the criteria for allocating concessional resources, with mixed results. On balance, the assessment was that introducing vulnerability indicators presented significant challenges, notably data constraints and lack of consensus on trade-offs, and the approach was ruled out after a long period of research... In sum, developing a new vulnerability index to access concessional resources would be impractical and not necessarily beneficial for all small states.*[103]

Other major multilateral development agencies mirror this approach, pledging support to the "most needy," and then excluding vulnerability from that assessment. International Monetary Fund mechanisms, like its Rapid Credit or Exogenous Shocks facilities have also limited their utility in post-disaster or post-crisis relief because they, too, exclude vulnerability from their assessment criteria:

> *In 2006, and Exogenous Shocks Facility was also created for [Poverty Reduction and Growth Facility]-eligible countries to provide concessional financing at ten-year maturity to meet temporary balance of payments difficulties caused by external shocks, including natural disasters. Currently, therefore, most of the Pacific island economies, as well as Dominica, Grenada, St Lucia, and St Vincent and the Grenadines in the Caribbean, and the Maldives in the Indian Ocean would be eligible for concessional assistance under these facilities. There is a clear question whether, given the incidence of natural disasters that affect all small states and the high indebtedness of many*

of them, concessional assistance for natural disasters, as well as the ESF, should be extended to all of them.[104]

Further, the IMF itself has conceded that "small states benefited much less than larger countries from the 2015-16 reforms to access under [Poverty Reduction and Growth Trust] facilities and the [Rapid Financing Instrument], and they find current access limits constraining in relation to their large balance of payments needs for the most severe disasters".[105] These limits, which are capped by islands' minuscule GDP-based Special Drawing Rights at the IMF, simply ignore the element of vulnerability. There are numerous examples of continued callous indifference to this fundamental characteristic of islands' anatomy and outlook.

These arbitrary rules mean that two island nations, less than one hundred miles apart, may have two different levels of access to concessionary financing. Or that two archipelagos, equally low-lying, and equally vulnerable to catastrophic hurricanes and sea level rise, face two completely different prospects for adaptation financing or post-disaster recovery.

It makes no sense.

The intensification of climate change and the fossilisation of globalisations' inequities have caused island nations to advocate increasingly for formal recognition of vulnerability as a crucial element of the developmental equation. Various vulnerability indices have been proposed and debated by academics. However, bureaucratic inertia and empty institutional patronising threaten to relegate vulnerability to a clichéd political talking point that is meaningless in the shaping of developmental policy or the allocation of scarce resources.

The issue is too central to small islands' developmental aspirations to suffer such a fate.

Islands cannot continue to have their developmental narrative shaped from outside and subjected to considerations of what is convenient or palatable to others. Vulnerability matters. Within the framework of the existing economic and political apparatus, it is impossible to overstate the importance of vulnerability as a prism through which to view developmental progress.

Islands can and must insist upon — or create — a measure of vulnerability that captures the specificities of their developmental struggles. They must then agitate for that measure to be meaningfully considered in the analyses and allocations that inform international cooperation.

There are limits to which islands can accommodate themselves to the inequities of the system in which they are expected to survive. There are limits to the types of arbitrary considerations that can be used to divide island states that share similar goals and challenges. There are limits to who tells the story of islands' struggle and how that story must be told.

Ironically, in islands' political interactions with the outside world, shared vulnerability is a source of strength. Islands become more vulnerable when their vulnerability is ignored.

CHAPTER EIGHT

Large Ocean Developing States

Big ship sailing on the ocean
We don't need no commotion

- Freddie McGregor

The Caribbean is an immense ocean that just happens to have a few islands in it. The people have an immense respect for it, awe of it.[106]

- Derek Walcott

V ery rarely, small island states become the unintended beneficiaries of global rule-making. There is probably no better
example than in the decisions that have greatly expanded
the maritime space over which islands have exclusive economic control. The decisions made over how this potential ocean wealth is controlled, conserved and exploited can dramatically alter small islands'
developmental path.

On 28th September 1945 United States President Harry Truman issued proclamations 2667 and 2668, which radically altered the
marine space that nations sought to control. Proclamation 2667 declared that:

> *Having concern for the urgency of conserving and
> prudently utilizing its natural resources, the Government
> of the United States regards the natural resources of
> the subsoil and sea bed of the continental shelf beneath
> the high seas but contiguous to the coasts of the United
> States as appertaining to the United States, subject to its
> jurisdiction and control.*[107]

Proclamation 2668, Truman's second edict that day, exerted US
control over fishing on the high seas:

> *In view of the pressing need for conservation and
> protection of fishery resources, the Government of the
> United States regards it as proper to establish conservation
> zones in those areas of the high seas contiguous to the*

> *coasts of the United States wherein fishing activities have been or in the future may be developed and maintained on a substantial scale.*[108]

At the time, Truman's Proclamations represented a breathtaking expansion of how much of the "high seas" states considered under their control. Before then, states exercised sovereignty over a narrow strip of coastal waters — traditionally the 3-nautical mile range of a cannon shot. Beyond that was an unregulated area known as the high seas. To claim jurisdiction over the continental shelf, which could extend for hundreds of miles, or to presume the authority to regulate fishing on the high seas, was unheard of.

It is important to consider the timing of Truman's Proclamations. The United States was weeks beyond its triumph in World War II, a position of global dominance that gave it licence for such unilateral action. The nation was also, naturally, concerned with its post-war coastal security. A separate proclamation, issued two weeks before 2667 and 2668, had discontinued maritime control areas along the eastern coast of the United States as "no longer necessary in the interests of national defence".[109] The United Nations Charter was still a month away from coming into force, and the Law of the Sea bodies it spawned did not yet exist. The technology for undersea oil exploration was maturing, and the United States was keen to extract the ocean's mineral wealth.

Most islands were still colonial territories.

Other nations quickly followed the United States example. In 1947, Chile and Peru asserted control over 200 nautical miles of seascape,[110] with Chile claiming "sovereignty over submarine areas, regardless of their size or depth, as well as over the adjacent seas extending as far as necessary to reserve, protect, maintain, and uti-lise natural resources and wealth". This declaration also established Chile's intention to establish "protection zones for whaling and deep sea fishery" extending 200 nautical miles from the coasts of Chile-an territory. Arab states, keen to protect their newly-discovered oil wealth, made a rapid series of similar declarations in 1949. By 1953, the United States had codified Truman's Proclamation in the Outer Continental Shelf Lands Act,[111] which declared:

> *the outer Continental Shelf is a vital national resource reserve held by the Federal Government for the public, which should be made available for expeditious and orderly development, subject to environmental safeguards, in a manner which is consistent with the maintenance of competition and other national needs;*[112]

After three decades of de facto ownership of ocean resources by the United States and other powerful nations, the 1982 meeting of the United Nations Convention on the Law of the Sea formally codified territorial waters of 12 nautical miles from the shoreline and an Exclusive Economic Zone (EEZ) of 200 nautical miles beyond that.

Island states, many of whom were just becoming independent nations, suddenly gained a massive juridical area. Barbados, an island with 166 square miles of land, has a marine territory of almost 71,000 square miles — over 400 times its land mass. Among pacific archipelagos, which are more widely dispersed than Caribbean islands, the maritime control area can be mind-bogglingly vast. Vanuatu's 80 islands add up to 4,700 square miles of land, and over 262,500 square miles of undisputed EEZ — a seascape larger than the land mass of France. The 33 islands of Kiribati are spread over a span of 1.4 million square miles of ocean. The 110,000 citizens of Kiribati can therefore lay claim to a seascape that is larger than India's land mass; or larger than the combined area of landlocked Ethiopia, Niger, Zimbabwe, and Botswana. Islands thus became the unintended legal beneficiaries of Truman's unilateralism. Considering these massive marine endowments, the very term "small island state" becomes a misnomer that reflects a land-based bias. Most Small Island Developing States could properly be construed as Large Ocean Developing States. With seabed mineral deposits of oil and polymetalic nodules, massive fish stocks, incredible biodiversity and world-class sailing and diving waters, these island states have potentially transformative developmental opportunities in the waters off their coastlines.

Colonising the Seas

However, the question of how to unlock the ocean's tremendous developmental potential remains unanswered. The resources necessary for proper management and sustainable exploitation of their vast seascapes remain beyond the capacity of all small island states. Islands' development partners have largely stood askance from state-led efforts to harness the transformative power of the oceans. Instead, they have advanced policies informed by paternalistic visions of subsistence near-shore "artisanal" livelihoods, or committed themselves to the neo-liberalisation of nature through privatisation and market-based environmental governance policies that bring only marginal benefit to the citizens most closely connected to the seas.[113]

Resource constrained islands — with no local fishing fleets, mineral exploration vessels, or means to police their vast ocean endowments — have found themselves in the unenviable position of peddling their ocean wares to rapacious global conglomerates on the most unfavourable terms. For example,

> [T]he Pacific tuna fishery for example accounts for close to two thirds of the value of the global tuna catch — some $4.3 billion. Yet the returns from their resource to Pacific islands is only around 2% of the catch value.[114]

Approximately 90 per cent of this Pacific tuna yield is harvested by distant-water fishing nations.[115] As such, the Pacific islanders benefit least in the global tuna value chain.

> Impressive though the catches of tuna from the South Pacific are, they have limited impact on the lives of the indigenous peoples of the region. Tuna are caught by highly mechanized industrial fleets of purse seiner, longline and pole-and-line vessels, often on the high seas. Less than 7% of this tuna is caught by Pacific island vessels and only 25% of the total landings is processed within the region.[116]

These dismal data are reproduced throughout island states. Similarly, islands with massive subsea mineral deposits rely on private companies to explore, map, mine, and process this wealth, often at the cost of multi-decade seabed leases at peppercorn rates. The leverage in these negotiations lies almost entirely with the capital-rich conglomerates. When Antiguan Prime Minister Gaston Browne charged that the cruise ship industry was "literally exploiting the Caribbean,"[117] major cruise company Carnival Cruise Line immediately and unilaterally cancelled all port calls to Antigua and Barbuda.[118] Neighbouring islands were only too happy to pick up the slack and lure Carnival to their ports.[119] The Chairman of the Organisation of Eastern Caribbean States, asked to comment on the kerfuffle instead posed a question:

> *Are we in such a state of servitude in the Caribbean that the prime minister cannot speak publicly in defence of what he perceives to be his country's interest without reprisals?... Unilateral reprisals. Is that where we are now? Is that old fashioned colonialism replaced by some new species of neo-colonialism?*[120]

The oceans that surround, separate, and connect islands have therefore yet to yield anything close to their potential developmental benefit. Oceans may define islands, but to date, they have also been a metaphor for islands' powerlessness to thwart rapacious exploitation by distant corporate interests. The Law of the Sea may have granted tremendous ocean resources to islands, but the far more powerful laws of neoliberal globalisation have thus far concentrated the oceans' benefits in distressingly familiar locales.

Blue Economy: Who Gets the Green?

The solution to this exploitative imbalance may lie in a concept that is rapidly gaining currency, if not clarity, in the international community: The Blue Economy.

However, the Blue Economy means different things to different people, with some interpretations posing tremendous developmental peril to island states. Small islands must therefore work to shape this concept in a manner that delivers the benefit of oceans to their citizens.

The 2012 Rio+20 Conference in Rio de Janeiro was held on the 20-year anniversary of the 1992 Earth Summit — formally called the United Nations Conference on Environment and Development — also held in Brazil. The 1992 Earth Summit, its 2002 follow-up and the Rio+20 Conference served to capture and codify international consensus on matters related to sustainable development and responsible environmental stewardship. At Rio+20, the concept of the Blue Economy was mooted as oceanic companion to the well-entrenched "Green Economy" strategy of deriving economic growth from land-based conservation and renewable energy initiatives. As a slogan, "Blue Economy" rapidly gained currency and acceptance, particularly among island and coastal states. Unfortunately, an agreed definition of the concept has proven more elusive. Blue Economy proponents alternately cite the concept as being related to small-scale fisherfolk, private sector-led exploitation and governance of ocean resources, marine conservation through enclosure, and establishment of "protected areas," creating ocean governance rules and ensuring that developing states receive a fairer share of ocean exploitation by private actors. Not all of these concepts are compatible with each other. Rather than confront these definitional contradictions, proponents of the Blue Economy have chosen to discuss rather than define; they sought to produce all-inclusive masterpieces of diplomatic jargon that encompass everyone's viewpoint:

> *At the core of the Blue Economy concept is the de-coupling of socioeconomic development from environmental degradation. To achieve this, the Blue Economy approach is founded upon the assessment and incorporation of the real value of the natural (blue) capital into all aspects of economic activity (conceptualisation, planning, infrastructure development, trade, travel, renewable resource exploitation, energy production/consumption).*

Efficiency and optimisation of resource use are paramount whilst respecting environmental and ecological parameters. This includes where sustainable the sourcing and usage of local raw materials and utilising where feasible "blue" low energy options to realise efficiencies and benefits as opposed to the business as usual "brown" scenario of high energy, low employment, and industrialised development models.[121]

Because of these ambiguities and contradictions, "it is not clear whether the term Blue Economy will come to be singularly understood as the domain of a particular set of actors (e.g., SIDS) or as a short-hand reference to particular sets of governance mechanisms (e.g., market based) or ideologies (e.g., the 'green economy')".[122]

Between the cracks of these definitional differences have sprung a number of concerning issues for island states. Chief among these have been the attempts to cede the exploitation of ocean resources to private, market-based concerns; and the move to sequester ocean resources while simultaneously imposing expensive management responsibilities on island governments. These and other concepts localise the "blue" while keeping the revenue "green" in the hands of distant private entities and global NGOs. Islands cannot allow their ocean resources to be shrunk or ceded to outside interests.

Global policies that purport to align the needs of the poor with profit interests and climate change concerns have proliferated in recent years. Since the 2012 Rio+20 conference, a number of ocean-centric "win-win" solutions for profit, people and planet have emerged. However, these policies and solutions have also been characterised as Trojan horses for the neoliberalisation of nature.[123] This neoliberalisation of nature is typified by

...a rapid increase in the involvement of private corporations in resource ownership, biotechnological innovation, and the provision of ecosystem services. Simultaneously, markets (and market proxies) have been deployed as mechanisms of environmental governance at

> *multiple scales... Opponents reject these developments as*
> *'greenwashing' of the appropriation of resources and*
> *the environmental commons for private profit, which will*
> *deepen socio-environmental inequities.*[124]

However altruistic their motivation, it is beyond dispute that NGO and private sector-led initiatives have appropriated millions of acres of islands' ocean and seabed resources in the name of conservation and marine protection. The management of these expansive conservation areas usually enjoys only nominal state participation. Other swaths of ocean real estate have been parcelled off to individual private sector entities for fishing, energy and tourism purposes. Some even see the hand of neoliberalisation at the level of individual animals, like the whale or the dolphin, where the emotional experience of close interaction with marine life is commodified for the benefit of private — and often foreign — tourism entities.[125]

In these unprecedented usurpations of islands' sovereign control of their ocean resources, the well-being of the residents of those islands is often a secondary consideration, beyond the promotion of some romanticised celebration of eking out a subsistence survival from low-wage, near-shore activity. It is not difficult to draw direct parallels between this foreign corporate imposition on ocean resources and the similar land-based response to many states' nationalist post-colonial policies. When control of nations' most valuable resources has been usurped by or ceded to foreign actors, it is appropriate to consider that loss of control though the prism of neoliberal or anti-imperial analysis.

Beyond the neoliberalisation of islands' ocean resources lies the unavoidable issues of who bears responsibility for both past ecological destruction and future environmental protection. The United Nations' *Blue Economy Concept Paper* baldly asserts that "[e]very country must take its share of the responsibility to protect the high seas".[126] But what does that mean? Does it mean that the 110,000 citizens of Kiribati — with a GDP of under US $200 million — bear responsibility to protect their 1.4 million square miles of ocean? That the

300,000 citizens of Barbados bear sole responsibility to superintend their Senegal-sized marine area? And what is the responsibility of the developed, industrialised nations whose carbon emissions, waste disposal and industrial exploitation have caused sea level rise and ecological damage in those same ocean areas?

Centuries of colonial, industrial and neoliberal exploitation of the natural environment have undoubtedly caused grievous ecological damage to oceans and fuelled climate change. The world's oceans play an indispensable role as "carbon sinks," reducing the concentration of greenhouse gases in the atmosphere and moderating the impact of CO_2 emissions.[127] Collectively, oceans are the world's largest carbon sink. Global warming and climate change would be much worse without their mitigating effort. As such, islands' role as custodians of vast swaths of oceans is indispensable in the battle against climate change. However, that role cannot be defined as being the modern-day dumping ground for industrialised nations' carbon trash, while simultaneously being constrained in their own use of ocean resources. If this were accepted,

> ...core or developed, industrialized regions [would be] able to shift their environmental burdens onto developing, or peripheral regions. The periphery, according to ecologically unequal exchange (EUE) theory, acts as 'source' of resources and planetary 'sink' for the metabolic needs of the core countries of the world-system.[128]

Clearly, such an unequal sharing of benefits and burdens is untenable. Islands' ocean territories cannot be expected to provide global benefits while tiny, cash-strapped countries bear the burden of maintaining or conserving that ocean space. Similarly, islands cannot be browbeaten into ceding sovereignty over marine territory as the only means of obtaining the resources necessary for conservation or development. Any discussion of the Blue Economy must therefore clearly delineate the lines of responsibility and action between today's largely blameless stewards of ocean resources and the historical role played by major exploiters and polluters. Any successful implementation of Blue Economy policies must be people-centric, island-focussed and developmentally driven.

The Blue (Destroyer of) Economies?

The giddy discussion of potential Blue Economy benefits is oftentimes divorced from the somber reflections on the destructive threat that oceans pose to islands. The potential of a warming, rising, raging ocean to destroy economic progress and development in small island states is more immediate and tangible than the still ill-defined benefits of the Blue Economy. Further, as sea level rise causes islands to disappear undersea, the size of archipelagos' marine endowments will correspondingly shrink as EEZs are recalculated according to surviving coastlines. This potential reduction in physical space under islands' control has its own implications for sovereignty, economic growth and political influence.

The ocean seascapes that house islands have double-edged developmental potential. Unfortunately, as the destructive edge of that sword is steadily sharpened by climate change, the obvious positive potential of oceans is blunted by ill-defined, paternalistic and neoliberal interpretations of the Blue Economy. Islands trapped in cycles of low or slow development are being denied opportunities to properly benefit from their immense ocean resources. This denial — fuelled by islands' capacity constraints, development partners' ideological blinders and corporate opportunism — must be collectively addressed by islands as the parameters of the Blue Economy are further delineated. Politically, islands cannot be shy to wield the size of their marine territory, their role as climate change mitigators, and the undeniable ecological debts of major polluters, to derive national developmental benefit for the peoples of their Large Ocean States.

Indeed, as the legal beneficiaries of President Truman's unilateral ocean grab seven decades ago, island governments should recall the parameters set forth by the United States 1953 Continental Shelf Lands Act. In defining the ocean space as a "national resource," held by the government for the benefit of its people, and to be utilised in the national interest for development albeit subject to environmental safeguards, Truman bequeathed a workable definition of the Blue Economy that should continue to serve as a template for islands' interaction with their oceans and the international community.

CHAPTER NINE

The Tyrannies of Indices

You Can't Study People

- Serani

In many spheres of human endeavor, from science to business to education to economic policy, good decisions depend on good measurement. More subtly, what we decide to measure, or are able to measure, has important effects on the choices we make, since it is natural to focus on those objectives for which we can best estimate and document the effects of our decisions[129]

- Ben S. Bernanke

One of the innovations of this era of short attention spans and instant analysis is list-making. The Internet is overcrowded with "top ten lists" and easily digestible rankings of everything from movies to meals. The thing near the top of the list is good, and the thing close to the bottom should be avoided. The developmental parallel to this facile fascination with classification is the "index". Every entity worth its salt spews forth some ranking that purports — through some complex and often opaque methodology — to compare apples, oranges, mangoes, and breadfruit.

Countries now find themselves on the Human Development Index, the Ease of Doing Business Index, the Corruption Perception Index, the Trafficking in Persons Index, the Press Freedom Index, the Human Freedom Index, the Economic Freedom Index, the Tourism Competitiveness Index, the World Happiness Index, the Gender Inequality Index, the Democracy Index, and the Where-to-be-Born Index, to name but a smattering. These indices are generated by a diverse assortment of academics, ideologues, do-gooders, governments and institutions, many of whom have real influence in shaping global perception. The rankings, when published, are dutifully reported by the press, highlighting the stand-out countries' performance. Local politicians and commentators cite the indices as either an accolade or a condemnation of whichever country they happen to call home. With each passing year, venerable indices gain greater currency, legitimacy and influence. Indeed, "[t]hose with long use have become naturalised, as well as hegemonic".[130]

Nowhere do these indices hold more sway than in Small Island States. Oftentimes, an index ranking is an outsider's first and lasting impression of a Small Island State. Investors shy away from unflattering doing business rankings, while the perception or support of multilateral institutions and foreign governments is coloured by an island's placement on this or that list. Worse, the "black list," the openly malicious kin of the seemingly-innocuous index, is specifically designed to name, shame and significantly increase the cost of doing business in enumerated states, a disproportionate number of whom are small islands. As a result, many small islands expend considerable resources on climbing a few notches up various arbitrary rankings. However, ironically yet unsurprisingly, the countries most affected by their placement on various rankings are those least involved in their creation, methodology or focus. Further, given the index-makers' own unfamiliarity with the small islands they purport to measure, and the fact that they rarely devote sufficient resources to updating, verifying or contextualising the underlying data, the picture that they paint of island states is incomplete at best, and often comically inaccurate.

Unfortunately, island states' inclusion on these rankings is oftentimes more a product of the drafters' desire to appear exhaustive and inclusive than it is reflective of any serious desire to accurately portray small island realities. The illusion of comprehensiveness is an important selling point in the legitimacy of the various indices and their parent organisations. That illusion is far more valuable than actual accuracy, especially to the instant-analysis consumers of these rankings. The fact that Small island states are less than a priority for the world's largest countries, institutions and NGOs is reflected in almost every aspect of the rankings — except in their actual impact on the perception of the islands themselves.

Indeed, the common critiques of these indices — that they are overly simplistic, devoid of context, arbitrarily weighted, opaquely determined, and deeply flawed as comparative tools — do not require regurgitation. It is instead the disproportionate impact of these indices on small island states, the resources required to improve national rankings, and the externally imposed perspectives, priorities and prescriptions that require particular focus.

Consider the issue of perspective. Of the 12 indices mentioned earlier in this chapter, five originate from Western European organisations, six from multilateral bodies headquartered in New York or Washington D.C., and one — the Trafficking in Persons Report — is generated by the U.S. State Department, which unashamedly gives its government top ranking for its fight against human trafficking, despite the voluminous and incontrovertible evidence to the contrary. Indeed, none of the indices rate their home country poorly. The Paris-based Reporters Without Borders places France within the top fifth of their annual World Press Freedom Index. The Economist Intelligence Unit, headquartered in London, bestows the United Kingdom with its highest ranking — "full democracy" — an accolade afforded only 20 nations in its Democracy Index. Germany annually hovers near the top 10 nations of the Corruption Perception Index generated by the Berlin-based Transparency International. The United States ranks similarly well on the Human Freedom Index, published by Washington D.C.'s Cato Institute.

And so on.

The standard-setting and agenda-setting influence of diverse indices generated in multiple large, developed, western, capitalist, neoliberal democracies is self evident. So too is the enforcement of normative behaviour through the negative sanction of low ranking. The transparently-veiled message — be like Germany! Be like France! Be like the United States! — is of particular concern to small island states whose history, demography, size, and socioeconomic characteristics could not be further removed from those of the countries they are being asked to emulate. The reinforcement of a perceived developmental hierarchy, viewed through the eyes of large, white, western, capitalist assessors, produces its own set of obvious challenges to the self-perception and policy decisions of states that exist beyond the parameters of this idealised norm.

The skewed developmental focus and cost is staggering. Small Island States with no history or evidence of human trafficking now set up elaborate, well-staffed anti-trafficking units within their police forces and commit their legislatures to enact harsh penalties against traffickers, all to improve their standing in the United States' Trafficking in Persons Report. Many of these small islands, lacking a single brothel, massage parlour, organised crime syndicate, or even international ports through which persons could be trafficked, nonetheless strive mightily to raise their arrest totals from zero to one and hold countless poorly-attended public education events in order to check the various boxes prescribed by the U.S. State Department. Similarly, the well-meaning but often unhelpful Doing Business Index published by the World Bank demands legislative and administrative focus on a set of externally-imposed priorities of dubious real-world utility in small island contexts. The unquestioning pursuit of ever-more-liberal bankruptcy laws by the governments of many Small Island States, for example, is almost entirely divorced from local demands or deficiencies and is an undisguised attempt to improve Doing Business rankings. Meanwhile, the lengthy and labyrinthine processes involved in simply opening a bank account — a far more practical and pressing impediment to doing business in most small island states — receives relatively scant official attention, because it does not contribute to the World Bank ranking and is not an issue in their Washington D.C. headquarters, where Bank economists can open checking accounts online in a matter of minutes.

Nonetheless, the uncritical and naked pursuit of improved ranking on the Doing Business hierarchy is a publicly-stated priority of most Small Island Developing States. For example, the Eastern Caribbean Central Bank, which sets monetary policy and strongly influences the developmental decisions of its eight small island members, has explicitly and unambiguously embraced ranking improvement as an immediate policy priority. In its 2017-2021 Strategic Plan[131], the Central Bank lists improving the Doing Business ranking of its members as a core priority, and baldly states, "As an institution, we have committed to support member countries to achieve a top fifty

(50) ranking on The World Bank's Doing Business Index[132]." Just like that, this external metric is not only accepted as a proxy for actual improvements in the local business climate, but its constituent areas of focus — and neglect — become mainstreamed into the developmental priorities of island microstates.

However, small island governments can scarcely be faulted for this ratings-specific resource commitment, because the development assistance decisions of the World Bank are coloured by its Doing Business determinations, to say nothing of the influence of the rankings on potential foreign direct investors. It is not uncommon for island states, making hopeful presentations to prospective investors or chambers of commerce from Dublin to Dubai, to be confronted with their Doing Business or Corruption Perception ranking as a seemingly insurmountable barrier to engagement.

Despite the ubiquity, popularity and influence of indices and index-making, it is telling that Small Island Developing States have been wholly unsuccessful in developing or facilitating the creation of ratings that would properly reflect small island specificities or properly contextualise their developmental needs and aspirations. For well over two decades, Small Island Developing States have collectively railed against the use of per capita GDP as the sole criterion for the measurement of wealth and determination of concessional development assistance. In the context of an island state with just a few hundred thousand citizens, per capita GDP is no more relevant a measure of wealth or developmental status than average individual dress size. The per capita GDP of The Seychelles or Antigua and Barbuda doubles that of the People's Republic of China, which begs the question of why those countries aggressively seek development assistance from China and not the reverse. Nonetheless, the per capita GDP measure persists as a rough-and-ready indicator of prosperity, driven by economists accustomed to dividing overall wealth by population denominators of tens of millions — or billions.

Small Island States have argued convincingly, and without demurrer, that any ranking of their developmental status and potential must take into account their numerous vulnerabilities and areas of resilience. These vulnerabilities include small size, susceptibility to natural disaster and climate change, economic openness, export concentration and over-reliance on a single productive sector, high dependence on strategic imports, debt burden, inequality, fixed costs related to remoteness, good governance, macroeconomic stability, and social development. In recent years, armed with voluminous academic research, the governments of Small Island Developing States have advocated the creation and use of a Vulnerability Index as a more accurate reflection of developmental status and a superior determinant of eligibility for concessional developmental assistance. Despite a number of polite and sympathetic hearings by the Bretton Woods institutions and major multilateral or bilateral players, a definitive Vulnerability Index remains beyond the reach of an indifferent international community, in spite of — or because of — the increased developmental havoc wrought by climate change on small islands. In the intervening 20 years of island advocacy on this issue, countless other less useful developed country ratings have emerged to place small island states in various shades of unflattering light.

The omnipresence of western data analyses and ratings, juxtaposed with the corresponding selectivity regarding what is measured and ranked, is of outsized significance to small islands' developmental path and sovereignty. The flattening of diverse national contexts and characteristics, under the guise of efficiency and comparison, threatens to vest excessive policy influence in the hands of faceless entities informed by a narrow set of ideological inclinations. In a world where a limited set of data are measured and quantified by a narrow set of analysts, power, influence and control of the developmental narrative will reside with the self-appointed scorekeepers.

Ultimately, the pursuit of improved placement in these rankings as an end in itself results in the tacit acceptance of a unitary and homogeneous developmental path, externally imposed, that ignores the complex specificities of individual states. The current crop of rankings represents an unsubtle institutionalisation of the one-size-fits-all philosophy that repeatedly draws the ire of Small Island Developing States.

Faced with this growing index tyranny, what are Small Island Developing States to do? The temptation to ignore the indices, and to chart a developmental path by ones own lights, completely divorced from the dictates of faceless foreign functionaries, is impractical. Rank ordering is undoubtedly crude, but it is an economical means of conveying information to those who need something less than an individualised, contextualised deep dive into the complexities of particular island states. The cruel irony is that the large, wealthy and well-known nations that produce these indices can afford to shrug off an unfavourable ranking. Small Island States, who neither produce, host, nor influence the underlying methodology of these indices, have no such luxury. For island states, major decisions and opportunities often rely, at least partially, on where their name appears on some arbitrary ranking.

Short of pretending that they don't exist, Small Island States seeking to loosen the grip of index tyrants have three overlapping options. One approach is to increase the validity of the rankings themselves by improving the quality of the data received by the adjudicators and by working with other states to improve the methodologies that govern the use and weighting of that data. While improving the quality of the data used to make rankings does not necessarily improve the quality of the rankings made from the data, the influence of these indices requires an improved commitment to accuracy and improved research. Very often, the ambition to produce a global index exceeds the available resources of the index-makers to ensure accuracy. Most often, it is small and peripheral states that suffer from these data-gathering failures. While the states themselves should try to ensure accuracy and provide timely statistical updates, the burden for accuracy lies with the self-appointed list-makers that purport to be the final word on the countries that they rank.

The corollary of data accuracy is methodological reform. Island states must collectively advocate improvements to the formulae and weighting of the data used to make rankings, and the assumptions that fuel those methodologies.

A second approach is to neither accept nor ignore the indices, but to oppose them, or at least attempt to contextualise their relative significance and shortcomings. This opposition should be consistently expressed and unrelated to whether a particular index happens to list a particular island state favourably. The challenges related to perspective, accuracy, methodology, context and oversimplification of complexities cannot be dependent on whether you are praised or damned in a particular ranking. Ultimately, despite their scientific trappings and statistical techno-babble, the existing crop of indices are not presentations of unvarnished data or facts. They are opinions. They represent the opinion of some small group of people that Norway is the most developed nation, or that New Zealand is the freest, or that Denmark is the least corrupt. Adjusting the formula by which these opinions are determined does not alter their status as highly subjective perspectives. The "aura of certainty" surrounding these rankings cannot obscure the fact that they represent opinions disguised as science. Further, they are opinions designed to reward or punish particular developmental decisions or priorities.

> The expansion of the use of indicators in global governance means that political struggles over what human rights or corporate social responsibility means and what constitutes compliance are submerged by technical questions of measurement, criteria, and data accessibility. Political debates about compliance shift to arguments about how to form an indicator, what should be measured, and what each measurement should represent.... The outcomes appear as forms of knowledge rather than as particular representations of a methodology and particular political decisions about what to measure and what to call it.... An indicator provides a transition from ambiguity to certainty; from theory to fact; and from complex variation and context to truthful, comparable numbers. In other words, the political process of judging and evaluating is transformed

into a technical issue of measurement and counting by the diligent work of experts.... Through the apparatus of science and measurement, the indicator displaces judgment from governing bodies onto the indicator itself, which establishes standards for judgment. Nevertheless, indicators are inevitably political, rooted in particular conceptions of problems and theories of responsibility. They represent the perspectives and frameworks of those who produce them, as well as their political and financial power. What gets counted depends on which groups and organizations can afford to count.[133]

The third approach, and one of particular importance for Small Island States, is to produce more rankings from sources beyond the current dominant poles of index generation that include or emphasise different criteria of greater validity in the small island context. Our decades long quest to emphasise vulnerability and resilience in developmental rankings should not end with the frustration of indifferent neglect by the major multilateral index generators. Small Island Developing States boast the University of the West Indies, the University of the South Pacific, countless research institutions from Cuba to Singapore to Mauritius, and a number of political gatherings like the Caribbean Community, the Pacific Islands Forum and the Alliance of Small Island States. Nothing prohibits us from producing and popularising a Vulnerability Index with the imprimatur of one or more of these respected indigenous institutions. Such an approach would not only challenge the western, large state, laissez-faire systemic bias, but would produce the first simplified, omnibus comparative ranking based on criteria of pressing developmental significance to Small Island States.

If you can't beat 'em, join em.

CHAPTER TEN

Black on the Blacklist

Babylon makes the rules, where my people suffer

- Steel Pulse

Still less, let it be proposed, that our properties, within our own territories, shall be taxed or regulated by any power on earth, but our own.[134]

- Thomas Jefferson

Most islands' first encounter with Western globalisation occurred when the caravels and galleons of European explorers dropped anchor off their shores. Those ships, and the ones that followed in their wake, quickly became vectors of disease, indigenous genocide, the trade in enslaved human beings, and colonial exploitation. The islands themselves became the far-flung objects of colonial design. They were administered from afar, their modes of production determined from a distance, and often, their very ownership changed hands as the result of great power intrigue in remote European capitals. While some colonies became very wealthy, the benefits derived from trade in goods between islands and colonial cities were decidedly slanted in favour of the poles of economic and military power in European capitals. The rules of engagement in the global trade in goods and services were written and designed in foreign capitals and enforced by royal fiat.

The more things change, the more they stay the same.

Today, one of the challenges of globalisation has been to establish a common set of enforceable rules governing the movement of people, capital, goods, and services, while also respecting the sovereign independence of individual states. Various multilateral mechanisms have been created to achieve consensus on these bedrock rules — from trade to banking to financial services — and to confront the problems wrought by modern globalisation, be they issues related to climate change, poverty or war and peace. However, these mechanisms have suffered from either a lack of inclusivity, transparency, arbitrary enforcement, or selective adherence by major world economies and powers. The brunt of each of these systemic failings is acutely felt by Small Island States, which are rarely consulted during the rule making process, and never powerful enough to influence, escape or ignore the impact of those rules. The result is that formal architecture of globalisation is designed without consideration for the needs of small island states and most often functions to their detriment. Despite small island states' best efforts to gamble on the fleeting loopholes, lacunae and grey areas in the ever-evolving rulebook of global casino capitalism, the house always wins.

However, small islands' challenges in navigating globalisation's treacherous currents have been compounded by advanced countries' simplistic and utterly false stereotypes of island businesses, governments and their developmental decisions. Indeed it is the stigma attached to island economies and sectors that pose the greatest developmental threat outside of climate change.

Islands are no strangers to facile stereotypes. Indeed, they have probably perpetuated a few of them. The popular image of dancing natives in bikinis or grass skirts welcoming visitors with broad smiles, an intoxicating cocktail and an introduction to the lazy, carefree ways of the local population is as much a creation of islands' tourist boards as it is the product of outsider misconceptions. However, while it may be possible to debate the relative merits of "positive" stereotypes in tourism and marketing, it is beyond dispute that small island developing states are ensnared in an insidious and erroneous lattice of vile stereotypes and assumptions that individually and collectively pose the threat of irreparably disrupting islands' already-tenuous participation in the global economy. These stereotypes, and the draconian responses that they inspire, have the potential to be self-fulfilling at best, and at worst, the basis of significant political, economic and developmental upheaval in small island states.

The modern stigmatisation of small island states portrays them as corrupt tax havens and welcoming homes for money launderers, fugitive criminals and a motley crew of international outcasts. Those stigmas have informed and been amplified by a series of increasingly aggressive blacklists designed to alter and ostracise island economies. The falseness of the blacklists' underlying stigmatisation itself is almost beside the point. As American political strategist Lee Atwater famously observed, "perception is reality". The reality of small islands' situation is that their collective stigmatisation has led to actions that have crippled investment, increased the cost of doing business, burdened local populations, and hobbled growth and development.

Life on the Blacklist

The use of blacklists by global rule makers is not a new phenomenon. Money-laundering blacklists, for example, have become commonplace over the last three decades. However, the September 11, 2001, terrorist attacks marked an inflection point in the use and weaponisation of blacklists as a tool for imposing sanctions beyond naming and shaming. Originally cast as a means to thwart the sort of terrorist financing revealed in the post 9-11 investigation, the focus of the Anti-Money Laundering/Combating the Financing of Terrorism (AML/CFT) regime have gradually shifted towards creating increasingly restrictive rules. Similarly, the 2008 financial and economic meltdown was blamed on insufficient regulatory oversight on financial institutions, which has led to an abundance of post-crisis rules and regulations. Curiously, these post-crisis rules aim at targets far removed from the epicenters of the crisis itself, as if the collapse of Lehman Brothers was precipitated by some wealthy businessman depositing a portion of earnings in a low-tax locale.

Perceived violations of those rules place nations on blacklists. The blacklists, in turn, spark sanctions and penalties that can grievously injure vulnerable economies. For example, banks that operate in countries that run afoul of the euphemistically-titled "standards" of the Financial Action Task Force (FATF) will have to add additional layers of expensive and time-consuming scrutiny to transactions involving blacklisted states. These costs are passed on to customers in affected countries. However, banks often simply stop doing business with those countries that reside persistently on the blacklists purporting to punish lax money laundering. Those banking decisions, in turn, can disconnect countries from the global financial system, and grind economies to a halt.

A separate set of standards and a different blacklist threat emanates from the United States' Foreign Account Tax Compliance Act (FATCA), which mandates banks around the world to report financial details of American's accounts and transactions to the U.S. Internal Revenue Service. Blacklisting for failure to comply attracts massive penalties and exponentially increases the threat of bank closure in the noncompliant jurisdiction.

Similar blacklists and penalties are applied by the European Union (EU) and the Organisation for Economic Co-operation and Development (OECD) in their ongoing crusade to eliminate so-called "non-cooperative tax jurisdictions". These non-cooperative tax jurisdictions, pejoratively known as tax havens, are often anything but. Their most common transgression is usually not responding with sufficient speed or docility to whatever new rule or procedure is determined to be the new litmus test of "tax cooperation". However, the consequences of EU/OECD blacklisting can be even more onerous than the FATF banking penalties. In addition to similar burdens imposed by banks on countries and customers, EU blacklisting allows for a host of financial sanctions against offending states. These include the withholding of tax revenues collected by EU states that are due to blacklisted entities, and freezing EU development grant funds or blocking of loans from the European development banks. For small island states, many of which rely on European developmental assistance, such sanctions have catastrophic potential. Ironically, in the aftermath of the WTO decision that obliterated banana exports to the United Kingdom, it was European authorities who encouraged island states to invest further in the financial services sector. Those same authorities are now openly hostile to the sector.

To say that the blacklisting and sanctions disproportionately affect small islands is an understatement. Oftentimes, the blacklisting is almost exclusively applied against small islands. For example, on 13

March 2019, the European Union published a blacklist of 15 alleged tax havens.[135] Of the 15 locales, 12 are members or associate members of the Alliance of Small Island States: Aruba, Barbados, Belize, Dominica, Fiji, the Marshall Islands, Samoa, Trinidad and Tobago, Vanuatu, and the three U.S. territories of American Samoa, Guam, and the U.S. Virgin Islands. A thirteenth so-called tax haven, the British overseas territory of Bermuda, is also an island and enjoys associate membership in the Caribbean Community (CARICOM). Only Oman and the United Arab Emirates, hardly large countries, found themselves in the company of these ostracised small islands.

Manufacture a Risk, then Avoid It

A major casualty of these island stereotypes, and their attendant blacklists, is correspondent banking relations. This era of blacklist proliferation and ever-changing compliance standards are a legislative burden for governments and an administrative nightmare for banks. Very often, banks determine that the risks of continuing to do business in tiny, fragmented island markets are outweighed by the compliance costs imposed by multiple reporting standards and the risk that they will be penalised for failing to adhere to those requirements. Banks' decisions to avoid, rather than manage, risk and thus "de-risk" by terminating or restricting business relationships with clients or countries is an increasingly prevalent part of the financial landscape of small islands.

The termination of correspondent banking relationships through the de-risking process is a grave and gathering threat to the economies of island states. Correspondent banking relationships are essential to enabling companies and individuals to transact internationally and make cross-border payments. Financial institutions in island states rely on correspondent banking relationships to provide access to the global financial system and underpin trade finance. As the Caribbean Development Bank recently explained:

> *Correspondent Banking Relationships (CBRs) exist between banks providing financial services (correspondent*

banks) and banks receiving those services (respondent banks). CBRs are fundamental to the efficient operation and resilience of the global financial system. They facilitate the re-allocation of capital, cross border payment systems and other services which are essential for international trade. CBRs also enable financial inclusion by providing to governments, corporations and ordinary citizens with access to a wide scope of globally networked financial services. In this way, they contribute immensely to the stability of the Caribbean's economic, financial and social ecosystem.[136]

As major international banks re-assess their exposure to risk and balance the cost of compliance against the profitability of their relationships with other institutions, a wave of CBR terminations has hit small island developing states, particularly in the Caribbean. Indeed, according to the World Bank, the Caribbean is the region "most severely affected" by the termination of CBRs as a result of de-risking. According to a November 2015 study by the World Bank, "89 percent of [Caribbean] jurisdictions reported experiencing significant to moderate declines in their foreign CBRs. Of the 19 respondent authorities, 15 reported significant declines and two others noted a trend towards decline or a moderate decline."[137]

The Caribbean Development Bank is more explicit in its chronicling of this trend.

Economically, the impact of the continued decline in correspondent banking on the Region has been substantial. Direct financial sector impacts include reduced business by banks and other financial intermediaries. For example, in Barbados, eight financial institutions have had their CBRs severed. Five of seven banks in Belize have had their CBRs terminated. In the Bahamas, two domestic banks and four international banks have also had their relationships brought to an end. In Haiti, all local banks have had their access to correspondent banking either severed or reduced. In the Eastern Caribbean Currency Union (ECCU), local banks that have maintained CBRs now have to pay significantly higher fees. Money Service Businesses (MSBs) such as, cambios in the case of Jamaica and money transfer services (Bahamas, Cayman Islands, Turks and Caicos Islands) have also been significantly impacted. In July 2015, Western Union closed its operations in the Bahamas and Cayman Islands.[138]

A study by the Commonwealth Secretariat explained how de-risking and loss of CBRs has already affected Belize.

[A]lmost all banks operating in the country have been affected by CBR closures or restrictions since Q4 2014, significantly impairing the ability of Belizean individuals and businesses to transact and trade internationally.

In 2016, two Belize banks lost their credit card settlement accounts in the USA. At the time of writing, these banks were unable to settle their credit card balances with payment systems operators, such as Visa, which insist on their customers using US bank accounts. These closures have had significant implications for the tourism industry in Belize as well as other international businesses operating from the country.

According to a recent Moody's Investors Service report (2016), '80% of Belize's banking system is likely to lose correspondent and credit card settlement services by mid-year 2016', with the loss of these services potentially disastrous for the country . . . Furthermore, if this trend continues, it could place significant pressure on central bank reserves, leading to potential credit default.

De-risking poses a serious threat not only to the banking and financial systems of Belize, but also to the operations of its monetary authority. The Central Bank of Belize lost one of its overseas accounts with a major international bank in 2016, impairing the country's ability to manage its official foreign exchange reserves, which are essential for ensuring foreign currency liquidity and absorbing external shocks in times of crisis.[139]

The Prime Minister of Belize has spent an inordinate amount of his time personally visiting banks and U.S. regulators, pleading with them to take his country's money.[140] Similarly, heads of government of Eastern Caribbean countries have made pilgrimages to financial capitals to engage banking managers in the hope that they will set aside preconceived stereotypes about island economies and instead engage on the basis of the region's well-regulated financial sector.[141]

De-risking and termination of CBRs is disproportionately an island phenomenon. According to the Financial Stability Board, which has been tracking the health of correspondent banking relations worldwide, "The most pronounced decreases between 2011 and 2017…were for Melanesia, Polynesia and the Caribbean."[142] Indeed, among Pacific and Caribbean islands, correspondent banks have been fleeing at a roughly equal rate.

Importantly, these de-risking exercises and accompanying terminations of correspondent banking relationships in small islands have generally not been as a result of regulatory breaches. However, many large international banks consider their business with small islands to be either high risk or unprofitable. With risk appetites declining in the wake of the 2008 global crisis, many financial institutions have opted to exit relationships assessed as being high risk, unprofitable, or simply "complex," such as those with money service businesses, foreign embassies, international charities, and correspondent banks. These financial institutions now have to maintain vast regulatory compliance departments that scrutinise every transaction to avoid massive penalties and fines. When they balance the cost of compliance against the small size and volume of transactions from relatively tiny banks, it is often cheaper — and certainly less risky — for the large institutions to simply terminate their relationship, no matter how well-regulated the local bank or financial sector may be. However, an international stamp of approval for a compliant financial sector is of little value to a country whose long-run growth and financial inclusion prospects are crushed by increasing costs of financial services and negatively affecting bank ratings.[143]

Break the Law to Make the Law

One of the features of modern globalisation is that its most far reaching rules and draconian punishments are conceived and enforced not through inclusive or representative intergovernmental bodies, but instead in closed, opaque groups of limited diversity. The small groups that make these global rules then apply them extraterritorially, using a series of oppressive tactics that violate the spirit, if not the letter of international law.

Consider the blacklists generated by the FATF, the OECD, the EU, and FATCA. The Financial Action Task Force has only 38 members, most of whom are also among the world's largest economies. The FATF members not among the world's top 38 economies consist of New Zealand and five European countries: Finland, Greece, Iceland, Luxembourg, and Portugal. Conversely, most of the countries among the 38 largest economies but excluded from full membership in the FATF — Colombia, Indonesia, Iran, Nigeria, the Philippines, Saudi Arabia, Taiwan, Thailand, and the United Arab Emirates — have a distinctly non-European background. The 36 members of the Organisation for Economic Co-operation and Development demonstrate considerable overlap with the FATF membership, with only six non-European countries not being a member of both groups. The membership of the European Union is, by definition, narrower than that of the FATF or OECD, but most EU countries are members of all three rule-making bodies. Other powerful rule-making entities, like the G20 and G7, as their names suggest, are even more restrictive. Most exclusive is the rule-making pursuant to the Foreign Account Tax Compliance Act, a law passed by the United States alone.

Conspicuous by their near total absence from these bodies are island states. With the exception of Singapore, whose powerhouse economy earned it a presence among the FATF membership, there are no islands present at the table when rules are formulated that affect them most profoundly. An island-inclusive intergovernmental body, like the United Nations, is mandated by its Charter to promote solutions to international economic issues and to study, report and make recommendations on economic matters to the international community.[144] However, the United Nations, and its Economic and Social Council, have been sidelined in the process of establishing the framework for globalisation's economic and financial rules.

This exclusion is by design. The world's western economic powers have zealously guarded their long-standing proprietorship over the levers of globalisation and the design of its supporting financial architecture. That design seeks to minimise the burdens of global movement of labour and capital while aggregating the greatest benefits to themselves. The European Union's famous tax haven blacklists, for example, target small islands while excluding EU member states that maintain massive low-tax and no-tax jurisdictions like Malta, Luxembourg and the United Kingdom.[145] European businesses, banks and tax attorneys escape major sanction while powerless, peripheral countries are intimidated and penalised to the point of economic ruin.

Further, the legal reach of the chummy decisions by overwhelmingly European and American rule-makers are extended extraterritorially in breathtaking examples of illegal international bullying. Under the American FATCA law, every nation on earth is mandated to act as an unpaid IRS informant, or face penalty. The European Union nonchalantly instructs states around the world to alter their tax laws to comply with a set of dictates dreamed up by European bureaucrats, and punishes those that fail to acquiesce within EU-determined timelines. These actions, no matter their motivations, represent a frontal assault on the time-worn, foundational principles of sovereignty and the attendant prohibitions against interfering in the internal affairs of independent states.

Undoubtedly, national boundaries have lost much of their relevance in today's business realities. Modern communication technology, the transnational structure of some corporations, and economic and financial globalisation raise complex questions about the principles that undergird the concept of the independent Westphalian nation state. But rather than addressing these complexities in an inclusive and cooperative manner, the small subset of wealthy, powerful nations has decided to cynically and hypocritically circumvent issues of extraterritorial law by strong-arming individual countries to enact blacklist-avoiding local legislation.

This trend of forcing countries to legislate at the barrel of a loaded blacklist reached its zenith in late 2018 as islands around the world kept their parliaments open over the Christmas holiday to hurriedly pass EU-compliant laws before an arbitrary January 2019 deadline. Unanimously decried as "hypocritical", "unconscionable" and "bullying" by a host of small island governments,[146] the parliaments nonetheless attempted to comply with the EU and OECD dictates in the face of certain blacklists and sanctions. Prime Minister Dean Barrow of Belize, presaging the impending capitulation to foreign legislative mandates, said:

> *Although we strongly disagree with what, dressed up in nice sounding arguments and fancy language, is nothing less than a hypocritical bushwhacking of our effort at economic diversification, we are powerless to do other than comply. It is still the way of the world that the small and weak are harried and bullied by the rich and the powerful. Thus, in order to avoid the destruction the industrialised world can visit on us by way of punishment, Belize has committed to have the necessary legislative amendments.*[147]

The threat of blacklisting and punitive sanctions are a powerful motivator. The FATF blacklist, for example, "has prompted international banks to move resources away from listed states and raised the costs of continued non-compliance, significantly increasing the number of states with laws criminalising terrorist financing".[148] However, the idea that a small group of powerful countries can gather together, agree upon rules that do not apply to them, and then apply those rules punitively against other states, runs counter to almost every agreed principle of international law and global governance. Yet the practice is picking up steam. Each year more blacklists proliferate, as do the number of increasingly arcane rules to which states must fastidiously comply. These rules, in the time-honoured tradition of overzealous bureaucratic mission creep, become progressively less applicable to the originally targeted evil, even as the penalties become more and more harsh. The brunt of those penalties is being borne disproportionately by small island developing states.

Whitewashing the Blacklist

Yet the blacklist is not inviolable. In early 2019, the EU published a new "dirty money" blacklist of purported money laundering jurisdictions that cast its net beyond the usual small island suspects. Apparently emboldened by their intimidatory muscle flexing against powerless countries, the dirty money blacklist was formed using separate criteria than the venerable FATF money laundering blacklist. Significantly, the EU's new blacklist included United States territories, as well as Saudi Arabia, a global economic power and major EU trading partner. But the blacklist's reach exceeded its grasp. The United States blasted the measure as ill-conceived, and its Treasury Department simply instructed banks to ignore the blacklist and the penalties it purported to impose.[149] Saudi Arabia also expressed its displeasure, dispatching a letter from King Salman bin Abdulaziz, ominously warning that the blacklisting would "create difficulties" in trade and investment flows between Saudi Arabia and Europe. Behind the scenes, Saudi diplomats threatened to cut ties with European capitals.[150]

Within days, the European Union was rescinding its blacklist, noticing for apparently the first time that it "was not established in a transparent and resilient process".[151] The dirty money blacklist was stillborn.

It is hardly novel to suggest that the blacklists are biased or that major powers like the United States and Saudi Arabia know how to throw their weight around to get what they want. However, the American and Saudi success in "unringing" the blacklist bell is instructive to small island states. The EU's "dirty money" debacle highlights two fundamental errors in islands' approach to blacklisting.

First, islands facing blacklisting have traditionally addressed the matter largely as an exercise to be resolved among technocrats; but in limiting their engagement to mid-level technical functionaries in the blacklisting bureaucracy, island states are tacitly accepting the bases, methodologies and overarching right of foreign capitals to impose extraterritorial control on distant countries. The Saudi opposition was diplomatic, not technocratic. They communicated at the levels of heads of state and between foreign ministers. At that level, the issue was stripped of its façade of technical neutrality and exposed as an imperialist incursion that would have consequences. It was this diplomatic *realpolitik* that yielded results. Similarly unhelpful are the highly technical discussions with the risk managers at banks that have terminated correspondent banking relations. Islands have to take the discussion up the ladder and cast it as a urgent developmental issue requiring a political fix.

Second, the success of the American and Saudi diplomacy highlights the other deficiency in islands' approach to date: a lack of unity. Historically, islands' most successful diplomatic forays have been made *en bloc*, with a united front that projects the strength and numbers necessary to effect change. Unfortunately, islands have not used this diplomatic muscle on the blacklist issue. Instead, individual islands have made isolated attempts to correct their specific perceived shortcomings and avoid blacklisting. Those islands temporarily spared from blacklisting have joined the advocacy of their condemned colleagues only half-heartedly, as if fearing the contagion of foreign sanction. Islands divided are islands conquered. Without the clout of America or Saudi Arabia, islands can only overcome blacklists collectively.

Yo Ho Ho and a Bottle of Rum

Since Port Royal's 17th century heyday as a pirate anchorage in Jamaica, islands have been stereotyped as isolated enclaves all too willing to help buccaneers hide their ill-gotten gains. That stereotype persists today, and fuels an unnatural focus on islands' activity as the scapegoat for all manner of perceived financial impropriety. While jurisdictions from Delaware to London to Malta to Luxembourg to Switzerland are treated with kid gloves, small islands with small economies are subject to a frontal assault by powerful countries. The prospect of repeated blacklists, and the threat of de-risking, have the real potential to devastate island economies. Imagine a tourist-based economy unable to process visitors' credit cards for accommodations, or a remittance reliant population unable to receive vital support from relatives abroad. Imagine businesses and investors unable to pay for purchases, import goods, or even establish bank accounts. The economic threat is existential.

Nonetheless, islands are fast reaching the point where the cost of compliance may soon outweigh the sanctions imposed by blacklist. If islands are repeatedly asked to legislatively scuttle all of their most profitable economic programmes to avoid blacklists — from online gambling to offshore banking to citizenship by investment — the question will ultimately arise as to whether the cure is worse than the disease.

As with other indicators, blacklists' legitimacy is derived from broad international support and acceptance. Island states must collectively begin the process of creatively challenging the bases of that international support and exposing the uneven stereotyping that takes global rule making from the realm of collective cooperation to Imperial imposition.

CHAPTER ELEVEN

Punching Above Our Weight

Small pin does chook hard

- Alston Becket Cyrus

We have heard a lot this afternoon about the word small. The United Nations is an organization of States, equal States, large and small. It is well known that in the United Nations there are many small countries that punch above their weight.[152]

- Kofi Annan

In 1967, U Thant, the then-Secretary General of the United Nations, gave voice to the concerns of large nations and great powers regarding the place of small and island states in international affairs. Identifying so-called 'microstates' like Nauru by name, the Secretary General stated "it appears desirable that a distinction be made between the right to independence and the question of full membership in the United Nations".[153] He fretted that the participation of small and island states in the business of the UN "may lead to a weakening of the United Nations itself," and he recommended that our engagement be limited to interactions with specialised bodies, or at best, observer status in the General Assembly.

Today, much has changed. The Alliance of Small Island States (AOSIS) boasts 37 full members of the UN, comprising one-fifth of the General Assembly. The sixty million inhabitants of Small Island Developing States represent the cultural, biological, historical, geographic, ethnic, and socioeconomic diversity of the world itself. Twenty-seven of AOSIS' 37 UN members have populations of under one million, and 17 of them have fewer than 250,000 citizens. Yet, despite their size, the contributions of small states have proven to be, in the words of another former Secretary General, Kofi Annan, "... the very glue of progressive international cooperation for the common good."[154]

However, the initial indifference, paternalism and outright antipathy towards small island states continue to lurk beneath the thin veneer of diplomatic formalities. The erroneous view that small island states should be observers, and not participants, in important matters of international relations is self-evident in islands' underrepresentation or outright exclusion from the inner sancta of decision-making bodies on international security, economic cooperation, development finance, and sustainable development. Those slights beg the question of whether some powerful states would prefer that small islands subsist as full members of the UN in name only, enjoying the legal fiction of sovereign equality, while remaining observers to a geopolitical drama in which islands can neither meaningfully act nor contribute to scripting the outcomes.

Fortunately, for once, the contradictions of a global order that was designed before and without islands' input has bequeathed them one potential advantage: a disproportionately high numerical presence in the international community, relative to their size and economic or military strength. For example, the 14 independent member states of the Caribbean Community (CARICOM) boast a mere .25% of the world's population, .09% of the planet's area, and .11% of the global GDP. Small fractions of one per cent. Yet, CARICOM controls over seven per cent of the votes at the United Nations, a pivotal bloc that is 25-60 times larger than their population, economy or land mass would suggest. The AOSIS voting bloc — at 20% of the UN membership — is potentially pivotal on a host of issues beyond their traditional focus on climate change.

Of course, international decision-making is rarely democratic. Major decisions are ported to opaque and non-representative bodies where decisions are made and enforced by powerful minorities. Within supposedly democratic bodies like the Organisation of American States or the United Nations General Assembly, the power of the vote is diluted by the entrenched pursuit of unanimous "consensus," and an institutionalised aversion to actual voting, thereby giving outnumbered major powers the ability to thwart or compromise the weight of majority opinion. Nonetheless, within the bodies that they participate, island states have the potential to wield considerable influence.

Influence as a Commodity

The grant of voting equivalence or theoretical diplomatic parity between China (population 1.4 billion) and Tuvalu (population 10,000) has often been cited as an anomaly of international relations. The relative weight of islands' votes, coupled with their limited developmental and revenue earning potential, have led to the stereotype-fuelled assumption that islands simply engage in crass transactional vote trading and are particularly susceptible to the unprincipled "dollar diplomacy" of wealthier nations. Academics have theorised that this active trade in "geostrategic rents" — foreign economic assistance in exchange for votes or other unearned political advantage — is a cornerstone of islands' developmental strategy.[155]

Undoubtedly, there are times when practical economic consideration, either by inducement or threat, factor into islands' diplomatic decision-making. Additionally, there is a fair argument to be made that island blocs — far from being passive pawns in a big-money diplomatic game — have occasionally inserted themselves into thorny disputes in ways that have secured them benefits. However, self-interested diplomacy is not the unique province of islands. Nor do those who bemoan the population disparity between islands and major powers typically draw attention to the fact that Indonesia seven times larger than Canada, or that the United Kingdom occupies a permanent seat on the United Nations Security Council, while India — with a population 21 times larger than the United Kingdom — does not. Further, with a few notable exceptions, the institutionalisation of aid has limited the extent to which politically-based bilateral assistance can have a transformative effect on island development.

More often, the stereotype of islands selling diplomatic support to the highest bidder is a product of shallow, stylised bias than it is of any empirical data.

Influence as Security

Indeed, there is ample evidence to suggest that islands have leveraged their perceived diplomatic advantages in the interest of more existential goals than mere commercial transactions. Island States, as creations of international law, have become unusually vociferous defenders of its principles. Issues of sovereignty, non-interference and non-intervention have a long and proud history of island advocacy. Islands' defence of international treaties and conventions — from the Law of the Sea, to accords on small arms control and climate change — demonstrates a greater faith in these precepts than is typically displayed by larger, more powerful nations. Just as domestic law protects the weak against the strong, so too does international law protect fragile states from intervention and interference by the mighty.

Sovereign equality of states, like many of the other legal fictions that undergird international law, enjoys, at best, a maddeningly inconsistent level of adherence and observance. However, this tenet, and the principle of non-interference by external actors, is of existential importance to small islands. Before resorting to high principles of international law, larger nations can hope to preserve their territorial integrity or political autonomy through some combination of wealth, military might, natural resource endowment, or geostrategic significance. For small islands, international law is the fig leaf under which our independence resides. Without it, small islands' existence depends on the whims, beneficence or benign neglect of larger powers.

Across Caribbean countries, for whom the proximity to the United States has always been a double-edged developmental sword, the long history of frequent American interferences in its perceived backyard has engendered a healthy appreciation for the practical importance of the esoteric legal principles of international law. The result is that, generally speaking, Caribbean states have proven to be unusually stout defenders of the principles of sovereign equality, non-interference and non-intervention. There have been, of course, embarrassing deviations from this defence, when the immediate and intense pressures of those with a hegemonic hunger for intervention have trumped high principle. But any analysis of actual or threatened interferences in the internal affairs of Cuba, Honduras, Nicaragua, El Salvador, Venezuela, Syria, Libya, Iraq, or Iran will find Caribbean countries at the vanguard of opposition or refusal to acquiesce to the interventionist imperatives of would-be hegemony — even when there is no direct bilateral connection between the countries. Similarly, Pacific island states are increasingly reluctant to endorse imperial statecraft.

It takes very little imagination to recognise that even a half-hearted economic blockade, or a few rhetorical broadsides from the leader of a major power, would be destabilising in a small island context. In most islands, where standing armies are either minuscule, ceremonial or non-existent, military intervention would be a fleetingly brief and one-sided affair.

Island states' staunch defence of foundational principles of the UN Charter — a document that, by and large, they played no role in drafting — can be seen through the prism of their own existential vulnerabilities. Oftentimes, islands' interpretation of these principles causes them to cross diplomatic swords with some of their strongest allies and benefactors. However, in arenas where islands' voices are valued numerically, the value of that numerical weight can be enhanced if it is not traded cheaply but rooted in a discernible pattern of consistent, principled conduct in international affairs.

Island states, always on guard against exclusion by decision makers, have always been the staunchest defenders and promoters of multilateralism. As global challenges proliferate, the need for global — that is to say, multilateral — solutions similarly increases. Islands have consistently stood on the principle that the fundamental wellspring of equitable multilateralism is mutual respect and a willingness to eschew short-term responses in favour of lasting, long-term solutions. In the island context, multilateralism and solidarity are the two indivisible sides of the same coin.

Institutionally, there is ample evidence to demonstrate lingering, long-standing biases against small island participation at the highest level of diplomatic decision making. Among the membership of the United Nations Security Council, for example, the unique perspectives of small islands are often absent — even when islands and island-specific issues are being debated. The UN Security Council has five permanent members — China, France, Russia, the United States of America and the United Kingdom — and 10 non-permanent members that are elected for two-year terms. Of the 37 small island states in the UN, only seven have ever served as non-permanent members of the Security Council: Cape Verde, Cuba, Guinea-Bissau, Guyana, Jamaica, Singapore, and Trinidad and Tobago. Ninety-five percent of the states serving on the Security Council have been non-small islands. Of the remaining states that have never served on the Security Council, almost half are small island states. Most of the time that the Security Council meets, there is not a single island state at the table. For 70% of its almost eight decade existence, the Council didn't have a single island among its membership. As the body has debated issues in Cuba, the Dominican Republic, Fiji, Guinea-Bissau, Haiti, Seychelles, Solomon Islands, and Timor-Leste, and tackled small arms, HIV/AIDS and Climate Change, the voice and view of islands has been troublingly excluded.

Even as the descendants of the indigenous, the enslaved, the indentured, and the coloniser have been forced to coexist on limited land masses with scarce resources, Islands have solved, often spectacularly, many of the ethnic and historical tensions that bedevil other nations. Out of necessity they have learned that the solution to conflict is not always more money or more military power. They have, embedded in their national psyches, a pragmatic love for peaceful problem-solving that the international community would do well to acknowledge and emulate. Islands have a lot to teach larger, more powerful nations about solutions to today's vexing global challenges. Increasingly, islands states must demand the attention of these larger states, force their way into the inner sancta of global decision making, and stand confidently on the principles that are central to islands' existence.

Little, but Talawah

In 2017, the United States attempted to use the Organisation of American States as a platform to gain diplomatic sanction for interventionist action against Venezuela. The initiative was blocked by a few tiny CARICOM states, citing the principles of sovereignty and independence. *Miami Herald* columnist Andrés Oppenheimer expressed bewilderment that "St. Vincent and Grenadines, a country whose gross domestic product of $751 million is less than the appraised value of the Fontainebleau Hotel in Miami Beach," could stand in the way of the United States' ambitions.[156] He considered it "ridiculous that the OAS voting system allows a handful of tiny islands to control the organisation's agenda". Seven years earlier, at the United Nations, CARICOM states — again citing issues of sovereign equality of states — led opposition to a European Union bid to enshrine itself as a pseudo-state within the UN structure.[157] A watered-down version of the EU's attempted power grab ultimately made it through the UN General Assembly, after protracted negotiations with the island nations. Four decades before that General Assembly vote, four Caribbean nations (Barbados, Guyana, Jamaica, and Trinidad and Tobago) — in their infancy as independent countries — defied crushing Cold War pressure to recognise and establish diplomatic relations with the socialist government of Cuba.[158] At the time, Errol Barrow, then Prime Minister of Barbados proclaimed his country "shall not involve ourselves in sterile ideological wranglings because we are exponents not of the diplomacy of power, but of the diplomacy of peace and prosperity". Warming to his subject, Barrow famously declared:

> It demonstrates that the developing countries can take a lead in conditioning the minds of people who should know better.... And I have no doubt that the other countries which are mightier and more powerful than the four small independent countries in the Caribbean will soon shamefacedly or not, have to follow suit.... We cannot sit down in the Caribbean and wait for our strategy to be dictated or governed by the political or other economic or social prejudices of people in other countries because to entertain such a belief would be an abandonment of the sovereignty that we believe in and we have never

subscribed to the doctrine of limited sovereignty. And I have been, myself, very firm right from the beginning of Barbados' independence that we would be friends of all and satellites of none.

While this principle is not always observed with the vigour and courage displayed by Barrow and his fellow leaders in 1972, it nonetheless animates the diplomacy of the Caribbean and most small island states. That diplomacy must be celebrated for its consistent strength more than its occasional weaknesses. For it is that diplomacy that has garnered and secured lasting benefits, not to be tallied in dollars and Euros, but rather as more fundamental entries in the ledger book: Survival, Influence, Respect.

CHAPTER TWELVE

A Word on Sovereignty and Independence

This island is mine

*- Skinny Fabulou*s

The problem with independence was not
the change in form, but the change in spirit.[159]

- José Martí

With the heroic exceptions of Haiti and Cuba, the histories of island states are bereft of those singular, defining independence moments. Rather than an ennobling, mythical period of resistance, when entire populations are galvanised into unifying action against a common oppressor, most islands' final independence moments were decidedly bureaucratic affairs. The colonial power of the day — distracted by internal politics, worn down by a swelling anti-colonialist tide internationally, questioning the lingering profitability of their post-emancipation outposts, and receiving growing and occasionally violent demands for greater services from the occupied territories' populations — simply acceded to islands' requests for independence. It was all a very civilised affair.

To be sure, islands' histories are replete with great acts of resistance and heroism. Queen Nanny of the Jamaican Maroons led enslaved Africans in a war against the British in the 18th century and secured treaties and autonomy from her oppressors. A few decades later, Paramount Chief Joseph Chatoyer fought a successful war against British forces in Saint Vincent that resulted in the hemisphere's first treaty between the United Kingdom and an indigenous people. Famous insurrections of enslaved Africans, labour riots and pitched political battles dot many islands' histories; but for most, national independence was granted, not taken. No wars were fought, no blood was shed. Colonised populations sometimes debated the timing of the independence request, or whether independence was even advisable. In Saint Vincent and the Grenadines, for example, politicians opposed to the 1979 independence request considered Vincentians "safe as sardines" in a colonial embrace that was at once suffocating and indifferent.

This lack of a defining, unifying mythology of independent struggle is sometimes claimed to result in an ambivalence to nationalism, patriotism and independence. There are, of course, exceptions and contradictions within this generalisation. However, those who claim to discern this insufficiency of patriotism suggest that our ancestors, be they the subjugated indigenous, the enslaved African, or the indentured labourer, were not deemed fit to attain full citizenship in the colonial state. The state itself, conceptually, was a colonial imposition on the population. Indeed, the state was most often, a despised tool and symbol of oppression. When the colonisers exited the stage, they were replaced by a middle class management committee lacking in anti-colonial fervour and content to perpetuate or incrementally adjust the policies of the departing oppressors. Most people felt no immediate, tangible difference in their lives, and thus no enhanced emotional connection to the independent state. As tourism became the dominant economic driver in many islands, the policies and posture of governments became increasingly focussed on welcoming, serving, entertaining, and reconfiguring the state itself to cater to tourist preferences and stereotypes. In that environment of institutionalised kowtowing to foreigners, the argument goes, the local resident's sense of citizenship was further attenuated.[160] The creeping importance of migration and remittances in the lives of many citizens left them further unmoored from their state and government.

The acute developmental challenges for independent island states in a hostile global environment have led some to consider whether it is better to eschew liberation and pursue progress as an autonomous, non-independent colonial appendage. Within this category of "small service-driven dependent island economy,"[161] reside islands that have decided to forego nationalism and independence, while generally outperforming their independent neighbours in many indices, largely as a result of colonial largess. Indeed, of late,

Island societies have been at the forefront in actually struggling to postpone or prevent independence, with considerable success to date.... Apart from Gibraltar (an enclave in any case) and Western Sahara, all 16 of the world's remaining "non self governing territories" on the UN's list — often referred to as "overseas territories" — are islands.[162]

Some academics have theorised that modern nationalism was generated by a desire to rectify unsatisfactory levels of local inequality. This connection between nationalism and benefit, rather than seeing nationalism as a good in and of itself, suggests that nationalist sentiment may dwindle in difficult economic times.[163] As such, even among already-independent states, there is a not-insignificant public sentiment that wonders whether it was all worth it. For example, in an opinion poll taken in Jamaica on its 50th anniversary of independence, a whopping 60% of Jamaicans said they would be better off as a colony.[164] In 2009, citizens of Saint Vincent and the Grenadines held a referendum to remove the British monarch as their head of state, along with other constitutional reforms. The proposed reforms were soundly defeated.[165]

From this seemingly-tenuous connection between islands and their sense of independence and nationalism, it may be little wonder that some governments have commoditised citizenship itself, selling passports to affluent foreigners who, for reasons both legitimate and illicit, seek alternative nationalities. For many, passport-selling is the end of the slippery slope for those who lack the patriotism or the imagination to conceive a feasible path for small island development within the context of the nation-state, either as individuals or as an integrated collective. For others, the sale of citizenship represents another step in the creeping stranglehold of neoliberalisation — whether even the national psyche and patriotism can be privatised, commoditised and marketed. However, in those islands states that encourage foreigners to "come as a visitor, leave as a citizen," the public debate has been less about the odious vulgarity of so-called "citizenship by investment" programmes, and more about the most effective use of the revenue windfall, avoiding the corruption that inevitably accompanies the schemes, resisting a race-to-the-bottom competition with other passport-sellers, and maintaining a sufficient veneer of respectability to avoid international legal crackdown.

When the value of citizenship is determined by fluctuating market forces, the question arises of how to value the related concepts of nationhood, sovereignty and self-determination.

Hegemony, Sovereignty and Globalisation

How can this apparent internal ambivalence to nationalism and independence be squared with island states' position on the vanguard of those mounting an aggressive and eloquent defence of sovereignty on the world stage? Why are efforts to deepen political integration among islands stymied by insistence that there be "no dilution of [their] pristine national sovereignty"?[166]

One answer may be that the academic discourse on attenuated island sovereignty is little more than stylised bunk. Another may be that political and class elites defend and promote island sovereignty to serve narrow goals unrelated to general public sentiment or interest. Yet another explanation suggests that the matter is complex, island-specific, and impossible to capture in any neat theorisation.

However, what is certain, and what shapes not only islands' perspectives on sovereignty but their general world view, is that they have been subject to more sustained and multifaceted assaults on their sovereignty than most other groups of states. Islands' presence in the perpetual cauldron of assaults on their right to exist has undoubtedly produced complex outcomes and outlooks in a delicate dance of resistance and accommodation to external pressure.

In 1996, Vincentian Prime Minister James Mitchell, frustrated at his country's status as a staging post for the American war on drugs, exclaimed, "We've surrendered our sovereignty.... We've given the U.S. all the cooperation in the world. What else do they want?"[167] At that time, as longtime victims of America's Monroe Doctrine, with the U.S. invasion of neighbouring Grenada a very recent memory, and as unwilling proxies for Cold War skirmishes, the Caribbean islands were well-acquainted with brutish disregard of their independence.

Occasional coarse heavy-handedness remains, like the United States' naked coercion of Jamaica to surrender its citizen Christopher "Dudus" Coke to American legal authorities without constitutionally prescribed due process. However, more common today are the insidious attacks on self-determination, alternately by subversive political operatives or by the apostles and enforcers of neoliberal globalisation.

The United States' Central Intelligence Agency has a documented history of attempting to subvert and alter democratic elections in the Caribbean, from Guyana to Haiti to Jamaica.[168] Recently, shadowy election "consultants" Cambridge Analytica and Strategic Communications Laboratories — ironically fuelled by citizenship by investment companies — also sought, with some success, to change the outcomes of sovereign elections in the Eastern Caribbean in exchange for the victors' commitment to style their sale of citizenship in specific ways.[169]

Economic assaults on independence via the Bretton Woods Institutions' external imposition of policy mandates — from the Washington Consensus to today's austerity-laced structural adjustment programmes — have long represented a usurping of islands' policy sovereignty by the Washington D.C. ideologues and economists. This forced economic management by unseen, unchecked, unelected foreigners has been supplemented by increasingly bold attempts to manipulate legislative processes and enforce extraterritorial law by the European Union, the OECD and the United States. These interventions and impositions led economist Norman Girvan to correctly observe that "[t]he reality is that insular independence has become largely shambolic and economic sovereignty an illusion".[170]

Islands' responses of accommodation and resistance have been too episodic and insufficiently strategic to effectively navigate these constraints on sovereignty. Whatever the antecedents to their independence, the continued survival of islands depends on their ability to make real the illusory nature of their shrinking sovereignty and convince their populations of the intrinsic values of citizenship and independence. The circumstances surrounding the formal granting of islands' independence may have been largely mundane, but the battles to preserve, expand and use that sovereignty have been anything but.

CONCLUSION

Another Way is Possible

And now we country facing its darkest hour
So our people need us today more than ever
But in our fight to recover, if ever you feel to surrender
It have one little thing that I want you always remember:
We could make it if we try just a little harder
If we just give one more try, life will be much sweeter

- Black Stalin

One must bear in mind the differences between two possibilities. First, there is the situation where there is a set of measures designed to ameliorate the worst effects of the present system while leaving the system itself intact. The second involves a set of fundamental changes which are possible because they reflect a changed world in which it is commonly accepted that economic activity must be managed to achieve equitable results for the majority of people and where the purpose of political activity is to provide the management on behalf of the majority of the people.[171]

- Michael Manley

I slands are being globalised, climatised and stigmatised to the outermost edges of the global periphery, and to the edge of their own existence as credible, viable nation states. Should islands resign themselves to a future of climate catastrophe, rising indebtedness, economic marginalisation, fiscal colonialism, economic predation and vulnerability, IMF trusteeship, energy dependence, and food dependence?[172] Or is it preferable "to become a consuming appendage of North America financed by remittances, drug transshipment, loans, tourism services, and offshore financial services, with the attendant implications for [island] culture and society?"[173]

Surely, another way is possible.

There is a convincing, and correct, argument to be made that the current international order and financial architecture — designed and refined in the distant capitals of large, powerful states — will never adequately accommodate the needs and specificities of island states. There is a compelling case to made that, in the face of myriad external, existential and unrelenting threats, islands must reject and reinvent the circumstances of their neglect and subjugation. When checking out that real situation, Bob Marley poetically argued that "it seems like total destruction's the only solution".

This is not that argument.

Despite the unassailable logic of such arguments, the prospect of taking up arms against that sea of troubles, and by opposing them, is Quixotic at best. There is a completeness to the indoctrination of the

current order, and the ensuing belief, without a scintilla of supporting evidence, that a peripheral post-colonial state can migrate into
the core of developed countries. Merely conceiving of an alternative
to this purported natural order requires both courage and energy.
The baseless belief in the correctness of the existing hierarchies
means that only a minority of the most affected countries would support sweeping changes to the system that affects them. Achieving
critical mass in support of revolutionary reform would necessitate
protracted internecine battles to even summon the will for systemic
change. Even then, the odds of success would be, to put it optimis-
tically, only slightly better than zero. Further, as former Guyanese
President Cheddi Jagan explained, "[a]ny real confrontation with
imperialism will result In counter attack — military, economic and
ideological".[174] The prospect of that counter-attack is unpalatable, to
say the least, to the small, splintered, vulnerable nations of the developing world. Karl Marx once observed that "Men make their own
history, but they do not make it as they please; they do not make it
under self-selected circumstances, but under circumstances existing
already, given and transmitted from the past."[175] The circumstances
of today's asymmetries between island states and the systemic levia-
thans it would have to slay dictate a different course.

These essays have suggested that the lives of small island citizens can be improved, and the developmental trajectory of small
island states can be enhanced, with pragmatic and plausible reforms
to the system, the ways in which islands interact, and how they view
themselves. To be sure, as Michael Manley said, "only the Third
World can develop itself. At most, therefore, the search for change in
the world system is to provide a set of arrangements more favourable to the Third World".[176] The same is true for islands, specifically.

As such, we begin with the realisation that islands are unique,
exceptional, and uncaptured by the descriptions and prescriptions
currently applied to their reality. Islands' characteristics and specificities; their constraints and possibilities; are *sui generis*, and must be
treated accordingly. Neither unimaginative academic nor bureaucrat-

ic inertia can justify any attempt to flatten island specificities into a simplified, homogenous whole.

Accepting those specificities means crafting specific responses to islands' needs and desires, albeit within the broad confines of the existing architectures. Islands' relationships with debt, development assistance and trade partners require urgent reform. These reforms cannot be one-sided or imposed from on high. Systemic imbalances require rebalancing on both sides of the global see-saw. Similarly, acknowledgment of islands' exceptional nature means that attempts to ignore inconvenient characteristics or penalise unique considerations with blacklists and sanctions must end.

Islands' interactions with the outside world, politically and commercially, require accommodations and exceptions based on size and vulnerability. Short-term economic survival is otherwise a fraught proposition.

Climate change, as a terrifyingly cross-cutting threat of existential proportions, is a recognised global challenge. But that challenge cannot sacrifice islands' existence on the altar of political or economic expedience. Islands, as the least responsible but most affected, must occupy a central place in the solutions and strategies being employed against this menace.

Finally, islands' diplomatic presence gives them the potential to exert a disproportionately large influence in multilateral affairs. Islands must attempt greater coordination of their diplomatic actions wherever possible, insist that global challenges are addressed through inclusive global fora, and wield their potential power selectively on issues of importance.

These modest suggestions are not beyond the capacity or imagination of islands. They can be achieved for islands' collective ennoblement. Of course, there are other transformative policy imperatives, ranging from strengthening institutions, to deepening regional integration, to harnessing the energy and creativity of youthful populations, to unleashing the power of Information Communication Technology as a developmental tool. The effectiveness of those imperatives, however, will hinge on the specificities of individual islands, and cannot be adequately discussed in a brief, generalist, pan-island publication.

Island Time

Over four decades removed from the initial hand wringing about the place of small island states in the international community, our ability to survive and thrive in the most difficult of circumstances has repeatedly confounded naysayers and challenged the mouldy conventional wisdom of great power politics. In a geopolitical and financial architecture designed before islands' decolonisation, and solicitous of size, economic wealth, or military might, the very existence of islands is a rebuke to those who first questioned their viability and then doubted their ability to navigate a rapidly globalising world. Islands' developmental path is people centred. It is creative. It has much to teach the world about respect for the environment, racial and ethnic harmony, and unstinting faith in the limitless potential of our populations. Small islands' challenges are many, but they are not insurmountable. They require only a willingness to understand islands' unique characteristics, vulnerabilities, and limitless possibilities; while maintaining a strong commitment to implement joint actions in accordance with those understandings.

To those trapped in the belief that more weapons are the answer to conflict, that more debt is the answer to poverty, or that more time is the answer to urgent climate crises, there is another way. It is the way of solidarity, genuine cooperation, and full understanding of the needs, peculiarities and contributions of each member of the global family. It is the way of honouring sovereignty and legitimacy as equals on the international stage, and as irreplaceable manifestations of distinct and authentic civilisations. The time for that other way is now.

Because of their openness and small size, the fortunes of small island states are reflective of, and responsive to the economic and developmental health of the global architectures in a way that no other group of states can claim. Islands are the barometer — the canary in the mineshaft — of the global economy and environment. Their development is not simply a discrete regional issue; it is inextricably intertwined and mutually dependent upon global development. As goes the world, so go the small island states. And vice-versa.

John Donne, a 17th Century poet, is probably best known today for his "Meditation XVII" which begins with the famous words *"No man is an island. . ."* The modern realities of our global village have shaped Donne's 17th Century meditations into a 21st Century geopolitical truth. Today, no island is an island. The waters that surround their shores offer neither solace nor security from myriad external maladies. Islands are innocent to the whims and winds of distant actors and events, but are affected nonetheless. However, the challenges faced by islands are not theirs to face alone. With that in mind, it is apt to revisit the words of Donne's "Meditation":

No man is an island entire of itself;
every man is a piece of the continent, a part of the main;
if a clod be washed away by the sea, Europe is the less,
as well as if a promontory were,
as well as any manner of thy friends or of thine own were;
any man's death diminishes me,
because I am involved in mankind.
And therefore never send to know for whom the bell tolls;
it tolls for thee.

In considering and shaping development cooperation in a still-evolving world order, the unique needs and vulnerabilities of small island states must occupy a special place on the global agenda. Not as an act of charity or as the result of moral suasion, but as a matter of justice, of logic, and of islands' inalienable right to develop and to exist.

END NOTES

1. V.S. Naipaul, Derrick Walcott, Arthur Lewis

2. Noam Chomsky, "Jubilee 2000," *Rogue States: The Rule of Force in World Affairs*, South End Press, Cambridge MA 2000 at p.107 (also available at https://chomsky.info/19980515/)

3. See, e.g., Jason Furman and Lawrence H. Summers, "Who's Afriad of Budget Deficits: How Washington Should End Its Debt Obsession," *Foreign Affairs*, March/April 2019 (https://www.foreignaffairs.com/articles/2019-01-27/whos-afraid-budget-deficits)

4. *See*, Richard Vague, "Government Debt Isn't the Problem—Private Debt Is," *The Atlantic*, 9 Sept. 2014 (https://www.theatlantic.com/business/archive/2014/09/government-debt-isnt-the-problemprivate-debt-is/379865/); Steve Keen, "Ignoring the role of private debt in an economy is like driving without accounting for your blind-spot," 14 March 2012 (https://blogs.lse.ac.uk/politicsandpolicy/ignoring-the-role-of-private-debt-in-an-economy-is-like-driving-without-accounting-for-your-blind-spot/); Berrak Büyükkarabacak and Neven Valev, "Credit Expansions and Banking Crises: The Roles of Household and Firm Credit," Andrew Young School of Policy Studies Research Paper No. 06-55, May 2006 (http://www2.gsu.edu/~econtv/credit_boom.pdf)

5. Matt Egan, "Donald Trump: I'm the King of Debt," CNN Business, 7 May 2016 (https://money.cnn.com/2016/05/05/investing/trump-king-of-debt-fire-janet-yellen/index.html)

6. Harper Neidig, "Trump: 'I've always loved debt," *The Hill*, 11 Aug. 2016 (https://thehill.com/blogs/ballot-box/presidential-races/291207-trump-ive-always-loved-debt)

7. International Monetary Fund, *World Economic Outlook: Coping with High Debt and Sluggish Growth*, Oct. 2012 at pp. 41-43 (http://www.imf.org/external/pubs/ft/weo/2012/02/pdf/c1.pdf)

8. (http://www.bloomberg.com/news/2013-01-04/imf-officials-we-were-wrong-about-austerity.html)

9. "No short cuts: Short-term austerity in the aftermath of a severe crisis may prove more painful than thought," *The Economist*, 27 Oct. 2012 (https://www.economist.com/finance-and-economics/2012/10/27/no-short-cuts)

10. Eric Zuesse, "The IMF Admits It Was Wrong About Keynesianism," *Business Insider*, 5 Jan 2013

(https://www.businessinsider.com/imf-admitted-their-economists-were-wrong-2013-1)

11. Brad Plumer, "IMF: Austerity is much worse for the economy than we thought," *The Washington Post*, 12 Oct. 2012 (http://www.washington-post.com/blogs/wonkblog/wp/2012/10/12/imf-austerity-is-much-worse-for-the-economy-than-we-thought/)

12. J. Gordon, I. Karpowicz, S. Lanau, J. Manning, W. McGrew, M. Nozaki, and M. Shamloo, "Greece: Ex Post Evaluation of Exceptional Access under the 2010 Stand-By Arrangement," International Monetary Fund, IMF Country Report No. 13/156, June 2013 (http://www.imf.org/external/pubs/ft/scr/2013/cr13156.pdf)

13. *See, e.g.*, Annie Lowrey, "I.M.F. Concedes Major Missteps in Bailout of Greece," *The New York Times*, p. B1, 6 June 2013 (https://www.nytimes.com/2013/06/06/business/global/imf-concedes-major-missteps-in-bailout-of-greece.html)

14. Luc Eyraud and Anke Weber, "The Challenge of Debt Reduction during Fiscal Consolidation," International Monetary Fund Working Paper 13/67, March 2013 (https://www.imf.org/external/pubs/ft/wp/2013/wp1367.pdf)

15. *See*, Government of the Commonwealth of Dominica, *Post-Disaster Needs Assessment, Hurricane Maria, September 18 2017*, November 2017 (https://reliefweb.int/sites/reliefweb.int/files/resources/dominica-pdna-maria.pdf)

16. *See*, International Monetary Fund, *World Economic Outlook: Challenges to Steady Growth.* Washington, DC. October 2018 at p. 157 (https://www.imf.org/~/media/Files/Publications/WEO/2018/October/English/main-report/Text.ashx?la=en)

17. *See, e.g.*, ReliefWeb, *Tropical Storm Erika – Aug. 2015* (https://reliefweb.int/disaster/tc-2015-000119-dma)

18. Maurice Bishop, "Imperialism is not invincible," Speech to the 6th Summit of the Non-Aligned Movement, 6 Sept. 1979, Havana Cuba (https://www.thegrenadarevolutiononline.com/bishspkimperialismisnotinvincible.html)

19. *See, e.g.*, Moody's Investor Service, *Issuer In-Depth: Government of St. Vincent and the Grenadines – B3 stable: Annual credit analysis*, 26 January 2019, p.12 (https://www.moodys.com/research/Government-of-St-Vincent-and-the-Grenadines-B3-stable-Annual-Issuer-In-Depth--PBC_1155402)

20. *See*, "Who's Afraid of Budget Deficits: How Washington Should End Its Debt Obsession," p. 88

21. *Ibid.*, pp. 92-93

22. *See*, Jubilee Debt Campaign, "The new debt crisis in the glob-

al South," March 2017 (https://jubileedebt.org.uk/wp-content/up-loads/2017/03/Debt-trap-media-briefing_03.17.pdf)

23. *See, e.g.,* Statement by Hon. Audley Shaw, 2010 Annual Meetings of the International Monetary Fund and the World Bank Group, 8 Oct. 2010 (https://www.imf.org/external/am/2010/speeches/pr43e.pdf); Statement by the Most Hon. Andrew Holness, Prime Minister of Jamaica at the General Debate of the 71st Session of the United Nations General Assembly, 23 Sept. 2016 (https://gadebate.un.org/sites/default/files/gastatements/71/71_JM_en.pdf); *See also,* Central Bank of Trinidad and Tobago, "Resolving Sovereign Debt Distress in the Caribbean: Towards a Heavily Indebted Middle Income Country (HIMIC) Initiative," Sir Arthur Lewis Institute of Social and Economic Studies 15th Annual Conference, April 2014 (https://www.central-bank.org.tt/sites/default/files/page-file-uploads/Final%20-%20Resolving%20Sovereign%20Debt%20Distress%20in%20the%20Caribbean.pdf)

24. *See, e.g.,* International Monetary Fund, "Debt Relief Under the Heavily Indebted Poor Countries (HIPC) Initiative," International Monetary Fund Factsheet, 8 Mar. 2018 (https://www.imf.org/~/media/Files/Factsheets/English/hipc.ashx)

25. *See,* The World Bank, "World Bank Country and Lending Groups," 2019 (https://datahelpdesk.worldbank.org/knowledgebase/articles/906519-world-bank-country-and-lending-groups)

26. Bruce Golding, "Statement by the Honourable Bruce Golding, Prime Minister of Jamaica, to the 63rd Session of the United Nations General Assembly, Friday 26 September 2008," 26 Sept 2008 (https://www.un.org/ga/63/generaldebate/pdf/jamaica_en.pdf)

27. *See,* Travis Mitchell, "Debt Swaps for Climate Change Adaptation and Mitigation: A Commonwealth Proposal," Commonwealth Secretariat Discussion Paper No. 19, March 2015 (http://thecommonwealth.org/sites/default/files/inline/Debt%20swaps%20for%20climate%20change%20adaptation%20and%20mitigation-%20A%20Commonwealth%20proposal%202015.pdf); Jwala Rambarran, Debt for Climate Swaps: Lessons for Caribbean SIDS from the Seychelles, *Social and Economic Studies,* Vol. 67 Nos. 2&3, University of the West Indies, June/Sept. 2018; Economic Commission for Latin America and the Caribbean (ECLAC), "ECLAC's Proposal on Debt for Climate Adaptation Swaps: A strategy for Growth and Economic Transformation of Caribbean Economies," CARICOM – UN High Level Pledging Conference: Building a More Climate-Resilient Community, Nov. 2017 (https://www.cepal.org/sites/default/files/news/files/nydbetreliefcaribbean-november2017.pdf); *See also,* Ban Ki-moon and Kamalesh Sharma, "Swapping national debt for action on climate change could be the solution we've

been looking for," *The Independent*, 8 Jan. 2016 (https://www.independent.co.uk/voices/swapping-national-debt-for-action-on-climate-change-could-be-the-solution-weve-been-looking-for-a6802561.html)

28. According to the International Monetary Fund, hurricane clauses, included in sovereign debt bond contracts, enable changes to the scheduled debt service payments upon the realization of an exogenous natural disaster event. Since the changes to the scheduled debt service payments are pre-defined in a contract, this reduces the probability that another debt restructuring will be triggered. The hurricane clause is designed to provide cash flow relief at a critical moment after a natural disaster event, when financing needs are greatest and new sources are scarce. Therefore, it enables countries to redirect funds intended for debt service to more immediate needs, reducing the economic impact of the natural disaster. *See, also,* Michele Robinson, "Introducing Hurricane Clauses Lessons from Grenada's recent experience A countercyclical financial instrument," Commonwealth Secretariat, 2016 (http://thecommonwealth.org/sites/default/files/inline/Introducing%20Hurricane%20Clauses.PDF)

29. C. L. R. James, *The Black Jacobins: Toussaint L'Ouverture and the San Domingo Revolution*, New York: Vintage Books, 1963

30. Bruce Golding, "Statement by the Honourable Bruce Golding, Prime Minister of Jamaica, to the 63rd Session of the United Nations General Assembly, Friday 26 September 2008," 26 Sept 2008 (https://www.un.org/ga/63/generaldebate/pdf/jamaica_en.pdf)

31. International Monetary Fund, "Press Release: IMF Executive Board Approves US$1.27 Billion Stand-By Arrangement with Jamaica," 4 Feb 2010 (https://www.imf.org/en/News/Articles/2015/09/14/01/49/pr1024)

32. *See, e.g.*, "Editorial: Another IMF Programme Worthwhile," *Jamaica Gleaner*, 16 April 2018 (http://jamaica-gleaner.com/article/commentary/20180416/editorial-another-imf-programme-worthwhile)

33. *See*, United Nations, "Monterrey Consensus of the International Conference on Financing for Development," 22 March 2002 (https://www.un.org/esa/ffd/wp-content/uploads/2014/09/MonterreyConsensus.pdf)

34. World Trade Organisation, "Doha WTO Ministerial 2001: Ministerial Declration," Document WT/MIN(01)/DEC/1, 20 Nov. 2001, at ¶2 (https://www.wto.org/english/thewto_e/minist_e/min01_e/mindecl_e.htm)

35. *Ibid*, at ¶35

36. *See* World Trade Organisation, "Draft Cancún Ministerial Text," Fifth WTO Ministerial Conference, 13 Sept. 2003, at ¶18 (https://www.wto.org/english/thewto_e/minist_e/min03_e/draft_decl_rev2_e.htm)

37. Stephen Castle, "Pact Ends Long Trade Fight Over Banan-

as," *The New York Times*, p. B3, 16 Dec. 2009 (https://www.nytimes.com/2009/12/16/business/global/16banana.html)

38. See, World Trade Organization, WT/DS285/R, "Measures Affecting the Cross-Brder Supply of Gambling and Betting Services: Report of the Panel," 10 Nov. 2004 (https://docs.wto.org/dol2fe/Pages/FE_Search/FE_S_S006.aspx?Query=(%40Symbol%3d+wt%2fds285%2f*)&Language=ENGLISH&Context=FomerScriptedSearch&languageUIChanged=true#)

39. Tom Miles, "Storm-battered Antigua asks U.S. to settle 12-year old WTO bill," *Reuters*, 29 Sept. 2017 (https://www.reuters.com/article/us-usa-antigua-wto/storm-battered-antigua-asks-u-s-to-settle-12-year-old-wto-bill-idUSKCN1C4165)

40. Andrew T. Guzman, Beth A. Simmons, "Power Plays and Capacity Constraints: The Selection of Defendants in World Trade Organization Disputes," *Journal of Legal Studies*, vol. 34 (June 2005) The University of Chicago (https://dash.harvard.edu/bitstream/handle/1/3153319/simmons_powerplays.pdf?sequence=2)

41. *See, e.g.*, Muzaka, V., & Bishop, M., "Doha stalemate: The end of trade multilateralism?" *Review of International Studies, 41*(2), 383-406. 2015

42. Norman Girvan, "Existential Threats in the Caribbean: Democatising Politics, Regionalising Governance," C.L.R. James Memorial Lecture, Cirpiani College of Labour and Comparative Studies, 12 May, 2011 (https://www.caribbeanreview.org/2017/08/existential-threats-in-the-caribbean/)

43. United Nations General Assembly, Resolution A/Res/25/2626, "2626 (XXV). International Development Strategy for the Second United Nations Development Decade," 24 Oct. 1970 (http://www.un-documents.net/a25r2626.htm)

44. Lestor B. Pearson, *Partners in development: report of the Commission on International Development*, New York, Praeger, 1969

45. *See*, United Nations Resolution A/RES/60/1, "2005 World Summit Outcome," 24 Oct. 2005, at ¶23 (http://www.un.org/en/development/desa/population/migration/generalassembly/docs/globalcompact/A_RES_60_1.pdf)

46. *See*, United Nations Resolution A/RES/63/303, "Outcome of the Conference on the World Financial and Economic Crisis and Its Impact on Development," 13 July 2009, at ¶28 (http://www.un.org/ga/search/view_doc.asp?symbol=A/RES/63/303&Lang=E)

47. See, United Nations Resolution A/RES/69/313, "Addis Ababa Action Agenda of the Third International Conference on Financing for Development (Addis Ababa Action Agenda)," 17 Aug. 2015 at ¶51 (http://

www.un.org/en/development/desa/population/migration/generalassembly/docs/globalcompact/A_RES_69_313.pdf)

48. *See, e.g.*, United Nations, *The Sustainable Development Goals Report 2018*, New York, 2018, at pp. 13, 30 (https://unstats.un.org/sdgs/files/report/2018/TheSustainableDevelopmentGoalsReport2018-EN.pdf)

49. *See, e.g.*, United Nations Sustainable Development Solutions Network, *Investment Needs to Achieve the Sustainable Development Goals: Understanding the Billions and Trillions*, 12 Nov. 2015 (http://unsdsn.org/wp-content/uploads/2015/09/151112-SDG-Financing-Needs.pdf); *see also*, Aaron Maascho, "U.N. conference agrees on plan to finance development goals," Reuters, 16 July 2015 (https://www.reuters.com/article/us-africa-development/u-n-conference-agrees-on-plan-to-finance-development-goals-idUSKCN0PQ21D20150716); *See also*, Peter Thompson, "Opening remarks of H.E. Peter Thomson, President of the UN General Assembly at High Level SDG Action Event '*SDG Financing Lab*,'" 18 April 2017 (https://www.un.org/pga/71/2017/04/18/opening-of-sdg-financing-lab/)

50. *Investment Needs to Achieve the Sustainable Development Goals: Understanding the Billions and Trillions*, at pp 120-121

51. Economic Commission for Latin America and the Caribbean (ECLAC), "The Inefficiency of Inequality," Thirty-Seventh Session of ECLAC, Havana, May 2018 at p. 37 (https://repositorio.cepal.org/bitstream/handle/11362/43443/6/S1800058_en.pdf)

52. *See, e.g.*, William Easterly, Aart C. Kraay, "Small States, Small Problems? Income, Growth, and Volatility in Small States," *World Development*, Vol. 28 No. 11, Feb. 2000, pp. 2013-2027. (also available at http://documents.worldbank.org/curated/en/731471468766821640/pdf/multi-page.pdf)

53. Godfrey Baldacchino, "Bursting the Bubble: The Pseudo-Development Strategies of Microstates," *Development and Change*, 24(1) Jan. 1993 (https://core.ac.uk/download/pdf/46604125.pdf)

54. Baldacchino, p. 40 (internal citations omitted)

55. Godfrey Baldacchino, "Small Island States: Vulnerable, Resilient, Doggedly Perseverant or Cleverly Opportunistic?" *Études Caribéennes*, at ¶3, April–August 2014 (internal citations omitted) (http://journals.openedition.org/etudescaribeennes/6984)

56. *Ibid.*

57. *See*, Wim Naudé, "Entrepreneurship is not a Binding Constraint on Growth and Development in the Poorest Countries," United Nations University World Institute for Development Economics Research (UNU-WIDER) Research Paper No. 2009/45, Helsinki Sept. 2009 (https://www.econstor.eu/handle/10419/45166); Wim Naudé, "Entrepreneurship and economic

development: Theory, evidence and policy," United Nations University World Institute for Development Economics Research (UNU-WIDER) Working Paper No. 2012-027, Helsinki April. 2012 (http://collections.unu.edu/eserv/UNU:162/wp2012-027.pdf); Wim Naudé, "Promoting Entrepreneurship in Developing Countries: Policy Challenges," United Nations University World Institute for Development Economics Research (UNU-WIDER) Policy Brief No. 4 2010 (http://collections.unu.edu/eserv/UNU:2933/unu_policybrief_10_04.pdf); *See also,* Dan Senor and Saul Singer, *Start-up Nation: The Story of Israel's Economic Miracle,* Twelve, 2009

58. Frantz Fanon, The Wretched Of The Earth. New York : Grove Press, 1963.

59. Okun, Arthur M. *Equality and Efficiency, the Big Tradeoff.* Washington: The Brookings Institution, 1975

60. Bowles, Samuel. *The New Economics of Inequality and Redistribution.* Federico Caffè Lectures. Cambridge: Cambridge University Press, 2012

61. Stiglitz, Joseph E. The Price of Inequality: How Today's Divided Society Endangers Our Future. New York: W.W. Norton & Co, 2012.

62. Jonathan David Ostry & Andrew Berg & Charalambos G Tsangarides, 2014. "Redistribution, Inequality, and Growth," IMF Staff Discussion Notes 14/02, International Monetary Fund.

63. Jonathan D. Ostry, Andrew Berg, Charalambos G. Tsangarides, "Redistribution, Inequality, and Growth," International Monetary Fund, Staff Discussion Note 14/02, April 2014 pp. 8, 26 (https://www.imf.org/external/pubs/ft/sdn/2014/sdn1402.pdf)

64. Economic Commission for Latin America and the Caribbean (ECLAC), "The Inefficiency of Inequality," Thirty-Seventh Session of ECLAC, Havana, May 2018 at p. 15 (https://repositorio.cepal.org/bitstream/handle/11362/43443/6/S1800058_en.pdf)

65. Holy Bible, Matthew 26:11

66. Andrew G. Berg, Jonathan D. Ostry, "Inequality and Unsustainable Growth: Two Sides of the Same Coin?" International Monetary Fund Staff Discussion Note, 8 April 2011 (https://www.imf.org/external/pubs/ft/sdn/2011/sdn1108.pdf)

67. Joseph Stiglitz, "Inequality and Economic Growth," *Political Quarterly,* 2016 p. 149 (https://www8.gsb.columbia.edu/faculty/jstiglitz/sites/jstiglitz/files/Inequality%20and%20Economic%20Growth_0.pdf)

68. "Inequality and Unsustainable Growth: Two Sides of the Same Coin?" p. 16

69. *See,* "Goal 10: Reduced Inequalities," United Nations Development

Programme (https://www.undp.org/content/undp/en/home/sustainable-development-goals/goal-10-reduced-inequalities.html)

70. "The Inefficiency of Inequality," p. 25

71. Facundo Alvaredo, Lucas Chancel, Thomas Piketty, Emmanuel Saez, Gabriel Zucman, "World Inequality Report 2018," World Inequality Lab, 2018 at p. 11 (https://wir2018.wid.world/files/download/wir2018-full-report-english.pdf)

72. See, Joseph Stiglitz, "Inequality and Economic Growth," Political Quarterly, 2016 p. 135 (https://www8.gsb.columbia.edu/faculty/jstiglitz/sites/jstiglitz/files/Inequality%20and%20Economic%20Growth_0.pdf)

73. John Maynard Keynes, *The General Theory of Employment, Interest and Money*. London, Macmillan, 1936 at Chapter 24

74. Arthur W Lewis, 2003[1955] *The Theory of Economic Growth*. New York: Routledge, p. 376.

75. William G. Demas, *The Economics of Development in Small Countries, With Special Reference to the Caribbean*, University of the West Indies Press, 2009 pp. 96-98

76. *See, e.g., The Parliamentary Debates (Hansard)*, Fifth Session Eighth Parliament, Saint Vincent and the Grenadines, 25 Jan. 2010 at p. 58 (http://www.hansardsvg.com/styled/downloads-3/files/25th%20January%202010.pdf)

77. *Holy Bible*, Joshua 9:23

78. Mark Blyth, (2015). *Austerity: The history of a dangerous idea*, Oxford University Press, 2015

79. Mariana Mazzucato, *The entrepreneurial state: debunking public vs. private sector myths*, Anthem Press, 2015

80. *See, e.g.*, Ralph Gonsalves, "Addressing On-Going Socio-Economic Challenges Consequent Upon The International Economic Crisis," 2009, p. 4 (http://pmoffice.gov.vc/pmoffice/images/stories/Speeches/addressing%20on-going%20socio-economic%20challenges.pdf)

81. Fidel Castro, "The NATO plan is to occupy Libya," Reflections by Fidel, 21st Feb. 2011 (http://en.cubadebate.cu/reflections-fidel/2011/02/21/nato-plan-is-occupy-libya/)

82. Richard Black, "Ban Ki-moon tells Copenhagen summit to 'seal a deal,'" *BBC*, 15 Dec. 2009 (http://news.bbc.co.uk/2/hi/science/nature/8414798.stm); "Ban entreats leaders to seal climate deal on final day of Copenhagen talks," *UN News*, 18 Dec. 2009 (https://news.un.org/en/story/2009/12/324732-ban-entreats-leaders-seal-climate-deal-final-day-copenhagen-talks); Harvey Morris, "Ban Ki Moon: 'Seal the deal' battlecry to secure legacy," *Financial Times*, Sept. 20, 2009 (https://www.ft.com/content/

74b1a058-a3e9-11de-9fed-00144feabdc0)

83. "Lima call for climate action," Dec. 2014 (https://unfccc.int/files/meetings/lima_dec_2014/application/pdf/auv_cop20_lima_call_for_climate_action.pdf)

84. *See, e.g.*, Alexander White, "Sorry policy-makers, the two-degrees warming policy is likely a road to disaster," *The Guardian*, Sep. 9 ,2014 (https://www.theguardian.com/environment/southern-crossroads/2014/sep/09/new-york-climate-summit-two-degrees-warming-policy-disaster)

85. "Climate Change 2014 Synthesis Report," 2015 (https://www.ipcc.ch/report/ar5/syr/)

86. "Global warming of 1.5°C: An IPCC Special Report," Intergovernmental Panel on Climate Change, Jan. 2019 (https://www.ipcc.ch/site/assets/uploads/sites/2/2018/07/SR15_SPM_version_stand_alone_LR.pdf)

87. United Nations Framework Convention on Climate Change, "Report of the Conference of the Parties on its fifteenth session, held in Copenhagen from 7 to 19 December 2009, Part Two: Action taken by the Conference of the Parties at its fifteenth session," FCCC/CP/2009/11/Add.1, 30 Mar. 2010 at ¶8 (https://unfccc.int/sites/default/files/resource/docs/2009/cop15/eng/11a01.pdf)

88. *Ibid.*

89. *See*, United Nation, "Paris Agreement," 2015 (https://treaties.un.org/doc/Treaties/2016/02/20160215%2006-03%20PM/Ch_XXVII-7-d.pdf)

90. United Nations Framework Convention on Climate Change, "Summary and recommendations by the Standing Committee on Finance on the 2018 Biennial Assessment and Overview of Climate Finance Flows," Nov. 2018 (https://unfccc.int/sites/default/files/resource/51904%20-%20UNFCCC%20BA%202018%20-%20Summary%20Final.pdf)

91. OECD, "2020 projections of Climate Finance towards the USD 100 billion goal: Technical Note," OECD Publishing, 2016 (https://www.oecd.org/environment/cc/Projecting%20Climate%20Change%202020%20WEB.pdf)

92. *See, e.g.*, Leslie Hook, "Wealthy nations fall short of climate funding pledge," *Financial Times*, 23 Nov. 2018 (https://www.ft.com/content/cbce4e2e-ee5b-11e8-89c8-d36339d835c0); Mike Ives, "Rich Nations Vowed Billions for Climate Change. Poor Countries Are Waiting." *The New York Times*, 10 Sept. 2018 p. A10 (https://www.nytimes.com/2018/09/09/world/asia/green-climate-fund-global-warming.html); Patpicha Tanakasempipat,"Developed nations not committed to $100 billion climate finance: experts," *Reuters*, 5 Sept. 2018 (https://www.reuters.com/article/us-climat-

echange-accord/developed-nations-not-committed-to-100-billion-climate-finance-experts-idUSKCN1LL1CX)

93. *See*, Paris Agreement, Art. 9 ¶4; Copenhagen Accord, ¶ 8

94. "Summary and recommendations by the Standing Committee on Finance on the 2018 Biennial Assessment and Overview of Climate Finance Flows," p. 8

95. Copenhagen Accord, ¶8

96. "Summary and recommendations by the Standing Committee on Finance on the 2018 Biennial Assessment and Overview of Climate Finance Flows," p. 4

97. *See, e.g.*, Leslie Hook, "UN's flagship green finance fund fights to regain credibility," *Financial Times*, 22 Jan. 2019 (https://www.ft.com/content/7d22d8ca-0ea5-11e9-b2f2-f4c566a4fc5f); Alister Doyle, "Green Climate Fund meeting 'disappointing', chief quits," *Reuters*, 4 July 2018 (https://www.reuters.com/article/us-climatechange-gcf/green-climate-fund-meeting-disappointing-chief-quits-idUSKBN1JU2GR); Jess Shankleman, "UN's Green Climate Fund at 'Low Point' After Director Resigns, *Bloomberg*, 4 July 2018 (https://www.bloomberg.com/news/articles/2018-07-04/un-s-green-climate-fund-at-low-point-after-director-resigns); Joe Lo, "Why can't poor countries access the climate finance they were promised?" *The Guardian*, 15 Feb. 2016 (https://www.theguardian.com/global-development-professionals-network/2016/feb/15/small-island-states-green-climate-fund); Fatima Arkin , "At the UN's Green Climate Fund, the honeymoon is over," *Devex*, 10 July 2018 (https://www.devex.com/news/at-the-un-s-green-climate-fund-the-honeymoon-is-over-93093)

98. The World Bank Group, "The Costs to Developing Countries of Adapting to Climate Change – New Methods and Estimates: The Global Report of the Economics of Adaptation to Climate Change Study," World Bank, 2010 (http://siteresources.worldbank.org/EXTCC/Resources/EACC-june2010.pdf)

99. UNEP, "The Adaptation Gap Report 2018," United Nations Environment Programme (UNEP), Nairobi, Kenya, Dec. 2018, p. xiii (https://wedocs.unep.org/bitstream/handle/20.500.11822/27114/AGR_2018.pdf?sequence=3)

100. "The Costs to Developing Countries of Adapting to Climate Change – New Methods and Estimates: The Global Report of the Economics of Adaptation to Climate Change Study"

101. *See*, Rob Merrick, "Brexit secretary Dominic Raab says he 'hadn't quite understood' importance of Dover-Calais crossing," *The Independent*, 8 Nov. 2018 (https://www.independent.co.uk/news/uk/politics/

brexit-latest-dominic-raab-trade-eu-france-calais-dover-economy-finance-deal-a8624036.html); Aidan Radnedge, "Dominic Raab ribbed for 'Britain is an island' bombshell," *Metro News*, 9 Nov., 2018 (https://www.metro.news/dominic-raab-ribbed-for-britain-is-an-island-bombshell/1303114/); Rafael Behr, "Has nobody told Dominic Raab that Britain is an island?" *The Guardian*, 8 Nov. 2018 (https://www.theguardian.com/commentisfree/2018/nov/08/dominic-raab-britain-island-ignorance-brexit-secretary)

102. Emily Shugerman, "Donald Trump says Puerto Rico is 'an island surrounded by big water,'" *The Independent*, 29 Sep. 2017 (https://www.independent.co.uk/news/world/americas/us-politics/donald-trump-puerto-rico-hurricane-maria-comments-island-big-water-a7975011.html); Steve Benen, "Trump: Puerto Rico is 'an island surrounded by … big water,'" MSNBC, 29 Sept. 2017 (http://www.msnbc.com/rachel-maddow-show/trump-puerto-rico-island-surrounded-big-water);

103. The World Bank Group, "Small States: Vulnerability and Concessional Finance: Technical Note," The World Bank Operations Policy and Country Services (OPCS) July 2018, pp. 11, 27 (http://pubdocs.worldbank.org/en/339601536162647490/Small-States-Vulnerability-and-Concessional-Finance-Public-Disclosurev2.pdf)

104. Dinesh Dodhia, *The Emerging Debt Problems of Small States*, The Commonwealth Secretariat, 2008 at p. 59 (http://www.keepeek.com/Digital-Asset-Management/oecd/commonwealth/economics/the-emerging-debt-problems-of-small-states_9781848598980-en#page1)

105. IMF, "IMF Policy Paper: Small States' Resilience To Natural Disasters And Climate Change – Role For The IMF," International Monetary Fund, Dec. 2016 (https://www.imf.org/external/np/pp/eng/2016/110416.pdf)

106. D. J. R. Bruckner, "A Poem in Homage To an Unwanted Man," *The New York Times*, p. C13, Oct. 1990 (https://www.nytimes.com/1990/10/09/arts/a-poem-in-homage-to-an-unwanted-man.html)

107. Government of The United States of America, "Proclamation 2667: Policy of The United States With Respect to the Natural Resources of the Subsoil and Sea Bed of the Continental Shelf," 28 Sept. 1945 (https://www.trumanlibrary.org/proclamations/index.php?pid=252&st=&st1=)

108. Government of The United States of America, "Proclamation 2668: Policy of The United States With Respect to Coastal Fisheries In Certain Areas of The High Seas," 28 Sept. 1945 (https://www.trumanlibrary.org/proclamations/index.php?pid=253&st=&st1=)

109. Government of The United States of America, "Proclamation 2663: Discontinuing the Casco Bay, Portsmouth, New Hampshire, Boston, Cape Hatteras, and Key West Maritime Control Areas," 11 Sept. 1945 (https://www.trumanlibrary.org/proclamations/index.

php?pid=248&st=&st1=)

110. *See*, Presidential Declaration Concerning Continental Shelf of 23 June 1947, *El Mercurio*, Santiago de Chile, 29 June 1947; Presidential Decree No. 781 of 1 August 1947, *El Peruano: Diario Oficial*. Vol. 107, No. 1983, 11 Aug. 1947

111. Outer Continental Shelf Lands Act, 7 Aug. 1953 (https://legcounsel.house.gov/Comps/Outer%20Continental%20Shelf%20Lands%20Act. pdf)

112. *Ibid.*, §3(3)

113. *See*, Mads Barbesgaard, "Blue growth: savior or ocean grabbing?" *The Journal of Peasant Studies*, 2018 45:1,130-149

114. Amanda Ellis: June 16, Oceans Day Panel 4, SIDS and Oceans: Building Resilience, Enhancing Social and Economic Benefits, *quoted in* Jennifer J. Silver, Noella J. Gray, Lisa M. Campbell, Luke W. Fairbanks, Rebecca L. Gruby, "Blue Economy and Competing Discourses in International Oceans Governance," *Journal of Environment & Development*, Vol. 24(2) 135–160 June 2015 (https://www.researchgate.net/publication/276169584_Blue_Economy_and_Competing_Discourses_in_International_Oceans_Governance/download)

115. Liz Petersen, "Governance of the South Pacific tuna fishery," *Pacific Economic Bulletin* Vol. 16 No. 2, Asia Pacific Press, Nov. 2001 pp. 63-76 (https://core.ac.uk/download/pdf/156664756.pdf)

116. P. Dalzell, T. J. H. Adams, N. V. C. Polunin, "Coastal Fisheries in the Pacific Islands," *Oceanography and Marine Biology: an Annual Review*, 1996, 34, 395-531 UCL Press, at p. 397 (https://www.researchgate.net/publication/279894123_Coastal_Fisheries_in_the_Pacific_Islands/download)

117. "PM: Cruise Association exploiting Caribbean," *The Daily Observer*, 26 Feb. 2019 (https://antiguaobserver.com/pm-cruise-association-exploiting-caribbean/)

118. *See, e.g.*, Gay Nagle Myers, "Carnival drops Antigua from itineraries," *Travel Weekly*, 15 Mar. 2019 (https://www.travelweekly.com/Caribbean-Travel/Carnival-drops-Antigua-from-itineraries); "BREAKING: Carnival Cruise Lines Pulls Out Of Antigua, More Cancellations Expected," *Antigua News Room*, 11 Mar. 2019 (https://antiguanewsroom.com/news/breaking-caribbean-cruise-lines-pulls-out-of-antigua-more-cancellations-expected/)

119. "As Carnival Cruise Line Pulls Out Of Antigua, USVI Sees Opportunity," *The Virgin Islands Consortium*, 17 Mar. 2019 (https://viconsortium.com/news-2/as-carnival-cruise-line-pulls-out-of-antigua-usvi-sees-opportunity/); "USVI capitalising on 'Carnival' exit from Antigua:

Looking to see how territory could benefit from the exodus," *Virgin Island News Online*, 17 Mar. 2019 (http://www.virginislandsnewsonline.com/en/news/usvi-capitalising-on-carnival-exit-from-antigua)

120. "Gonsalves on Carnival Cruise Lines: Is That Old Fashion Colonialism Replaced by Some New Species of Neo-Colonialism?" *Antigua News Room*, 17 Mar. 2019 (https://antiguanewsroom.com/news/gonsalves-on-carnival-cruise-lines-is-that-old-fashion-colonialism-replaced-by-some-new-species-of-neo-colonialism/)

121. United Nations "Blue Economy Concept Paper," Sustainable Development Goals Knowledge Platform, 15 Jan. 2014 (https://sustainabledevelopment.un.org/content/documents/2978BEconcept.pdf)

122. "Blue Economy and Competing Discourses in International Oceans Governance," p. 137

123. *See, e.g.*, Karen Bakker, "The Neoliberalization of Nature." In *Routledge Handbook of Political Ecology*, ed. G. Bridge, T. Perreault, and J. McCarthy, 446–56. London: Routledge, 2015; Nik Heynen, Paul Robbins, "The Neoliberalization of Nature: Governance, Privatization, Enclosure and Valuation," *Capitalism Nature Socialism* Vol. 16 No. 1 Mar. 2005; Rosaleen Duffy, "Nature-based tourism and neoliberalism: concealing contradictions," *Tourism Geographies*, 2015 17(4). pp. 529-543 (http://eprints.whiterose.ac.uk/107455/)

124. "The Neoliberalization of Nature," p. 446

125. *See, e.g.*, "Nature-based tourism and neoliberalism: concealing contradictions," pp 7-8

126. "Blue Economy Concept Paper," p.4

127. *See*, U. Siegenthaler, J. L. Sarmiento, "Atmospheric carbon dioxide and the ocean," *Nature*, vol. 365, pp. 119–125, 9 Sept. 1993; P. Landschützer, N. Gruber, D. C. E. Bakker, U. Schuster, "Recent variability of the global ocean carbon sink," *Global Biogeochemical Cycles*, 28, 927–949, 11 Sept. 2014 (https://agupubs.onlinelibrary.wiley.com/doi/pdf/10.1002/2014GB004853); Tim DeVries, Mark Holzer, Francois Primeau, "Recent increase in oceanic carbon uptake driven by weaker upper-ocean overturning," *Nature*, vol. 542, pp. 215–218, 9 Feb. 2017

128. Mariko Frame, "The Neoliberalization of Nature: The Highest Stage of Ecological Imperialism?" World Society, Planetary Natures Conference, Binghamton University, July 2015 (https://worldecologynetwork.files.wordpress.com/2015/08/frame-fomatted.pdf)

129. Ben S. Bernanke, "Economic Measurement," Speech to the 32nd General Conference of the International Association for Research in Income and Wealth, Cambridge, Massachusetts, 6 Aug. 2012 (https://www.federal-

reserve.gov/newsevents/speech/bernanke20120806a.htm)

130. Sally Engle Merry, "Measuring the World: Indicators, Human Rights, and Global Governance," *Current Anthropology*, Vol. 52, No. S3, April 2011, p. S92 (http://www.jstor.org/stable/10.1086/657241)

131. Eastern Caribbean Central Bank, *Strategic Plan 2017-2021*: Transforming the Eastern Caribbean Currency Union Together, Saint Kitts and Nevis, 2017 (https://www.eccb-centralbank.org/files/documents/Stategic_Plan/ECCB_Stategic_Plan_2017P2.compressed.pdf)

132. *Ibid*, p. 46

133. "Measuring the World: Indicators, Human Rights, and Global Governance," p. S88

134. Thomas Jefferson, "Draft of Instructions to the Virginia Delegates in the Continental Congress" (MS Text of A Summary View of the Rights of British America), July 1774 (https://founders.archives.gov/documents/Jefferson/01-01-02-0090)

135. Council of the European Union, "The revised EU list on non-cooperative jurisdictions for tax purposes – Council conclusions (12 March 2019)," Brussels, 12 Mar. 2019 (https://www.consilium.europa.eu/media/38450/st07441-en19-eu-list-oop.pdf)

136. Caribbean Development Bank, "Discussion Paper: Strategic Solutions to 'De-Risking' and the Decline of Correspondent Banking Relationships in the Caribbean," Barbados, 2016, at p. 4 (https://www.caribank.org/sites/default/files/publication-resources/DiscussionPaper_Solutions_De-RiskingCBRs-5.16print.pdf)

137. World Bank Group, *Withdrawal from Correspondent Banking; Where, Why, and What to Do About It*, Washington DC, Nov. 2015 at p. 14 (http://documents.worldbank.org/curated/en/113021467990964789/pdf/101098-revised-PUBLIC-CBR-Report-November-2015.pdf)

138. Toussant Boyce, Patrick Kendall, "Policy Brief: Decline in Correspondent Banking Relationships: Economic and Social Impact on the Caribbean and Possible Solutions," Caribbean Development Bank, Barbados, 2016

139. Robert Hopper, "Disconnecting from Global Finance De-risking: The Impact of AML/CFT Regulations in Commonwealth Developing Countries," Commonwealth Secretariat, London, 2015 at p. 9 (http://thecommonwealth.org/sites/default/files/inline/DisconnectingfromGlobalFinance2016.pdf)

140. See, Yeganeh Torbati, "Caribbean countries entangled by U.S. financial crackdown," Reuters, 12 July 2016 (https://fr.reuters.com/article/companyNews/idUKL1N19X1DD); "PM Barrow visits the USA to ad-

dress issues within the banking sector," The San Pedro Sun, 28 Jan. 2016 (https://www.sanpedrosun.com/business-and-economy/2016/01/28/pm-barrow-visits-the-usa-to-address-issues-within-the-banking-sector/)

141. See, e.g., "Monetary Council trip to Canada 'highly successful'," The St. Kitts & Nevis Observer, 3 Oct. 2017 (http://www.thestkittsnevisobserver.com/sourced-information/monetary-council-trip-to-canada-highly-successful/)

142. "FSB Correspondent Banking Data Report – Update," Financial Stability Board, 16 Nov. 2018 (http://www.fsb.org/wp-content/uploads/P161118-2.pdf) pp.6, 24

143. "Recent Trends In Correspondent Banking Relationships – Further Considerations," International Monetary Fund, 16 Mar. 2017 (https://www.imf.org/~/media/Files/Publications/PP/031617.ashx)

144. See, e.g., Charter of the United Nations, Articles 55, 62 (http://www.un.org/en/charter-united-nations/index.html)

145. See, e.g., Pedro Gonçalves, "EU mulls blacklisting its own Member States," International Investment, 12 Oct. 2018 (https://www.international-investment.net/internationalinvestment/news/3505790/eu-mulls-black-listing-member); Prem Sikka, "A tax haven blacklist without the UK is a whitewash," The Guardian, 7 Dec 2017 (https://www.theguardian.com/commentisfree/2017/dec/07/eu-tax-haven-blacklist-whitewash-west-imperialism-tackle-avoidance)

146. See, e.g., "EU accused of bullying small island and Caribbean states with hired ruffians," Searchlight, 28 Dec. 2018 (https://searchlight.vc/searchlight/front-page/2018/12/28/eu-accused-of-bullying-small-island-and-caribbean-states-with-hired-ruffians/); "Brantley criticizes EU for 'blacklisting' St Kitts-Nevis and other developing Islands," WIC News 24 Dec. 2018 (https://wicnews.com/caribbean/brantley-criticizes-eu-blacklisting-st-kitts-nevis-developing-islands-150114258/); "Statement By Prime Minister Mia Amor Mottley," Barbados Government Information Service, 21 Nov. 2018 (https://gisbarbados.gov.bb/blog/statement-by-prime-minister-mia-amor-mottley/)

147. Hon. Dean Barrow, Budget Speech For Fiscal Year 2018/2019 "Maintaining Steadiness; Consolidating Stability; Advancing Growth," 9 Mar. 2018, p. 18 (https://www.nationalassembly.gov.bz/wp-content/uploads/2018/03/Budget-Speech-2018.pdf)

148. Julia Morse, "Blacklists, Market Enforcement, and the Global Regime to Combat Terrorist Financing," International Organization, March 2019 (https://www.researchgate.net/publication/331558767)

149. See, Robbie Gramer, Keith Johnson, "The EU's Dirty Money

Blacklist: North Korea, Syria, and... Puerto Rico?" *Foreign Policy*, 15 Feb. 2019 (https://foreignpolicy.com/2019/02/15/european-union-e-u-money-laundering-black-list-u-s-territories-dispute-treasury-department-tax-evasion/); Michael Peel, Mehreen Khan, "US attacks EU money laundering blacklist," *Financial Times*, 13 Feb. 2019 (https://www.ft.com/content/dba2c2ca-2f84-11e9-ba00-0251022932c8); Samuel Rubenfeld, Daniel Michaels, "U.S. Rejects New European Dirty-Money Blacklist," *The Wall Street Journal*, 13 Feb. 2019 (https://www.wsj.com/articles/europe-adds-saudi-arabia-to-dirty-money-blacklist-11550075013)

150. Francesco Guarascio, "After Saudi king's letter, EU states move to block dirty-money list," *Reuters*, 28 Feb. 2019 (https://uk.reuters.com/article/uk-eu-saudi-moneylaundering/after-saudi-king-letter-eu-states-move-to-block-dirty-money-list-idUKKCN1QH211)

151. *See*, Pedro Gonçalves, "EU states block plan to add Saudi Arabia to money laundering blacklist," *International Investment*, 7 Mar. 2019 (https://www.internationalinvestment.net/news/4001249/eu-block-plan-add-saudi-arabia-money-laundering-blacklist); The Associated Press, "EU nations reject Commission money laundering blacklist," *The Seattle Times*, 7 Mar. 2019 (https://www.seattletimes.com/business/eu-nations-reject-commission-money-laundering-blacklist/)

152. "Secretary-General Highlights Regional Challenges, Potential for Cooperation, In Remarks at Inauguration of Barbados United Nations House," United Nations Press Release, 3 Jan. 2002 (https://www.un.org/press/en/2002/sgsm8089Rev1.doc.htm)

153. Introduction to the Twenty-second Annual Report, 15 Sept. 1967, A. Cordier and M. Harrelson (eds.), *Public Papers of the Secretaries General of the United Nations: U Thant*, vol. 7: 1965-1967 (Columbia University Press 1977) 573-4

154. United Nations Press Release SG/SM/6639, "Secretary General Lauds Role of Small Countries in Work of United Nations, Noting Crucial Contributions," Address of Secretary-General Kofi Annan to a joint meeting of the Uruguayan Parliament in Montevideo, 15 Juy 1998 (https://www.un.org/press/en/1998/19980715.sgsm6639.html)

155. *See, e.g,* "Clem Tisdell, "The MIRAB Model of Small Island Economies in the Pacific and their Security Issues: Revised Version," Social Economics, Policy and Development Working Papers, University of Queensland, School of Economics, 2014; Geoff Bertram "The MIRAB model in the twenty-first century," *Asia Pacific Viewpoint*, Vol. 47, No. 1, April 2006 (http://www.geoffbertram.com/fileadmin/publications/The_MIRAB_Economy_in_the_Twenty_First_Century.pdf); Bernard Poirine, "Should We Hate or Love MIRAB?" *The Contemporary Pacific*, Vol. 10,

No. 1 (SPRING 1998), pp. 65-105; Godfrey Baldacchino, Geoffrey Bertram, "The Beak of the Finch: Insights into the Economic Development of Small Economies," *The Round Table*, 98:401, 141-160, 2009 (https://doi.org/10.1080/00358530902757867); Godfrey Baldacchino, "Small Island States: Vulnerable, Resilient, Doggedly Perseverant or Cleverly Opportunistic?" *Études Caribéennes* 2014, (http://journals.openedition.org/etudescaribeennes/6984)

156. Andrés Oppenheimer, "Caribbean countries should be ashamed of supporting Venezuela at OAS meeting," *Miami Herald*, 22 June 2017 (https://www.miamiherald.com/news/local/news-columns-blogs/andres-oppenheimer/article157463039.html)

157. Leigh Phillips, "EU bid for more rights at UN suffers surprise defeat," *eu observer*, 15 Sept. 2010 (https://euobserver.com/foreign/30807)

158. *See, e.g.*, Fidel Castro Ruz, "Remarks on the occasion of the 30th anniversary of the establishment of diplomatic relations with Barbados, Guyana, Jamaica and Trinidad and Tobago," Havana International Conference Center, 8 Dec. 2002 (http://www.fidelcastro.cu/en/discursos/speech-marking-30th-anniversary-diplomatic-relations-barbados-guyana-jamaica-and-trinidad)

159. José Martí, "Nuestra América (Our America)," (Revised translation for the Centro de Estudios Martianos), Published in *El Partido Liberal* (Mexico City), 20 Jan. 1891 (http://www.josemarti.cu/publicacion/nuestra-america-version-ingles/)

160. Aaron Kamugisha, *Beyond Coloniality: Citizenship and Freedom in the Caribbean Intellectual Tradition*, Indiana Free Press, 2019

161. Mcelroy, Jerome & Sanborn, Katherine. (2005). The propensity for dependence in small Caribbean and Pacific islands. Bank of Valletta Review (Malta). 31.

162. Godfrey Baldacchino, Stephen A. Royle, "Postcolonialism and Islands: Introduction," *Space and Culture* 13(2) 140-143, 29 April 2010

163. See, e.g., Arvin W. Murch, "Political Integration as an Alternative to Independence in the French Antilles," *American Sociological Review*, Vol. 33, No. 4 Aug., 1968; Menno Boldt, "Intellectual Orientations and Nationalism among Leaders in an Internal Colony: A Theoretical and Comparative Perspective," *The British Journal of Sociology*, Vol. 33, No. 4 Dec. 1982; Peter Meel, "Towards A Typology Of Suriname Nationalism," New West Indian Guide vol. 72 no. 3 &4 1998 (https://www.researchgate.net/publication/41125732_Towards_a_typology_of_Suriname_nationalism/fulltext/0e608233f0c46d4f0acbb7d3/41125732_Towards_a_typology_of_Suriname_nationalism.pdf?origin=publication_detail)

164. *See*, "Bring back the British! Most Jamaicans say they would be better off ruled from London," *Daily Mail*, 30 Jun. 2011 (https://www.dailymail.co.uk/news/article-2009487/We-stayed-Britain-Shock-poll-reveals-60-Jamaicans-think-theyd-better-colony.html)

165. *See*, Associated Press, "St. Vincent: Voters Save the Queen," *The New York Times*, 27 Nov. 2009, p A18 (https://www.nytimes.com/2009/11/27/world/americas/27briefs-queen.html)

166. *See, e.g.*, Ralph E. Gonsalves, "Free Movement of Community Nationals, CCJ, Shanique Myrie, Community Law and Our Caribbean Civilisation," University of the West Indies Distinguished Lecture, Trinidad and Tobago 17 June 2014 (https://www.nowgrenada.com/wp-content/uploads/2014/06/Distinguished-Open-Lecture-by-Dr-The-Hon-Ralph-E-Gonsalves.pdf); "St Vincent PM blasts CARICOM," *Caribbean360*, 18 June 2018 (http://www.caribbean360.com/news/st-vincent-pm-blasts-caricom)

167. Larry Rohter "Caribbean Nations Find Little Profit in Aiding U.S. Drug War," *The New York Times*, 24 Oct. 1996, p. A13 (https://www.nytimes.com/1996/10/24/world/caribbean-nations-find-little-profit-in-aiding-us-drug-war.html)

168. *See e.g*, "Foreign Relations, 1964-1968, Volume XXXII, Dominican Republic; Cuba; Haiti; Guyana," US Department of State Archive, ¶¶ 370-441 (https://2001-2009.state.gov/r/pa/ho/frus/johnsonlb/xxxii/44659.htm); Gaiutra Bahadur, "CIA Meddling, Race Riots, and a Phantom Death Squad," *Foreign Policy*, 31 July 2015 (https://foreignpolicy.com/2015/07/31/guyana-cia-meddling-race-riots-phantom-death-squad-ppp/); UPI, "Manley says CIA engineered Jamaican elections," *United Press International*, 7 Mar. 1983 (https://www.upi.com/Archives/1983/03/07/Manley-says-CIA-engineered-Jamaican-elections/1563415861200/); Michael Manley, *Jamaica: Struggle in the Periphery*, Third World Media, Feb. 1983; Kevin Edmonds, "The CIA, the Cold War, and Cocaine: The Connections of Christopher "Dudus" Coke," The North American Congress on Latin America (NACLA), 14 July 2010, (https://nacla.org/news/cia-cold-war-and-cocaine-connections-christopher-%E2%80%9Cdudus%E2%80%9D-coke)

169. Ronald Sanders, "External interference in Caribbean elections is real," *Barbados Advocate*, 25 March 2018 (https://www.barbadosadvocate.com/columns/external-interference-caribbean-elections-real); Freddy Gray, "Revealed: Cambridge Analytica and the Passport King," *The Spectator*, 31 Mar. 2018 (https://www.spectator.co.uk/2018/03/revealed-cambridge-analytica-and-the-passport-king/); Juliette Garside, Hilary Osborne, "The passport king who markets citizenship for cash," *The Guardian*, 16 Oct 2018 (https://www.theguardian.com/world/2018/oct/16/the-passport-king-who-markets-citizenship-for-cash); "Caribbean Elections in the Age of

Cambridge Analytica: SCL, Cambridge Analytica's Caribbean History," *TeleSur*, 25 July 2018 (https://www.telesurenglish.net/news/Caribbean-Elections-in-the-Age-of-Cambridge-Analytica-SCL-Cambridge-Analyticas-Caribbean-History-20180726-0014.html); April Glaser, "How Shady Was Cambridge Analytica?" *Slate*, 29 Mar. 2018 (https://slate.com/technology/2018/03/cambridge-analyticas-work-in-the-caribbean-was-pretty-shady.html)

170. Norman Girvan, "Existential Threats in the Caribbean: Democatising Politics, Regionalising Governance," C.L.R. James Memorial Lecture, Cirpiani College of Labour and Comparative Studies, 12 May, 2011 (https://www.caribbeanreview.org/2017/08/existential-threats-in-the-caribbean/)

171. Michael Manley, *Up the Down Escalator: Development and the International Economy – A Jamaican Case Study*, Howard University Press, 1987, p.268

172. Norman Girvan, "Existential Threats in the Caribbean: Democatising Politics, Regionalising Governance," C.L.R. James Memorial Lecture, Cirpiani College of Labour and Comparative Studies, 12 May, 2011 (https://www.caribbeanreview.org/2017/08/existential-threats-in-the-caribbean/)

173. Witter, Micheal, "Consensus and Economic Development in the Caribbean." Presented to the Annual Conference on Economic Development, Eastern Caribbean Central Bank. St. Kitts, 2000.

174. Cheddi Jagan "The 3 Kinds Of Nationalizations Capitalist, Reformist And Socialist, Capitalist Nationalisation," *New World Journal*, Vol. V No. 4 (https://newworldjournal.org/volume-v-no-4/the-3-kinds-of-nationalizations-capitalist-reformist-and-socialist-capitalist-nationalisation/)

175. Karl Marx, Daniel De Leon, *The eighteenth Brumaire of Louis Bonaparte*, New York: International Pub. Co., 1898 (available at: https://www.marxists.org/archive/marx/works/1852/18th-brumaire/ch01.htm)

176. *Up the Down Escalator: Development and the International Economy – A Jamaican Case Study*, p.218

About the Author

Camillo Gonsalves is the Minister of Finance, Economic Planning, Sustainable Development, and Information Technology of Saint Vincent and the Grenadines. He served previous stints as the Minister of Foreign Affairs and the Permanent Representative of Saint Vincent and the Grenadines to the United Nations. Camillo has degrees in Journalism, Law and Global Affairs from Temple University, The George Washington University and New York University.

Made in the USA
Middletown, DE
03 April 2019